THE JUDAS PROJECT

INTERACTIVE VIDEO STUDY GUIDE

by

James H. Barden, Jr. & Emilija Barden

Published by
Barrington & Walstone, Publishers

THE JUDAS PROJECT
INTERACTIVE VIDEO STUDY GUIDE

Second Printing
June, 1996

Unless otherwise indicated, all scripture references quoted in this work are taken from the NAS Version of the Holy Bible.

Written by:
James H. Barden, Jr. & Emilija Barden

Published by Barrington & Walstone, Publishers
P.O. Box 959
Shallotte, N.C. 28459
USA

Toll Free: (888) 777-2671   Pin No. 5949

ISBN/SPCN 0005065011

Printed in the United States of America

Wilmington Printing Company
Wilmington, North Carolina

To
Our God
Who's Love Towards Us
Truly Surpasses
Our Own Understanding

And To You

May You Who Seek Him
Find Him
And Forever Abide
In
His Love

Promises Fulfilled

INTRODUCTION

"The Judas Project" is a motion picture suggesting the same series of events surrounding the last years of the life and ministry of Jesus Christ. The setting is present day, in order to better understand the dynamics at work during His ministry 2,000 years ago. It brings to light why some were not willing to follow and/or accept someone as their Lord and Savior/Messiah who looked and dressed like an ordinary man.

Jesus Christ was God in the flesh and He would not conform or bow down to the spirit of religiosity that constantly confronted Him. Would it be any different today?

Our goal in writing the Interactive Video Study Guide is to weave the study guide, screen play, video and bible together, interactively, in such a way as to:

• Bring out the humanity of Jesus. Present Him as touchable and reachable ... someone you could walk with and talk with. He was a man who knew how to laugh, throw His arms around you and embrace you...and yes, He even knew how to cry.

• Show the heart of Jesus... His love and compassion.

• Bring out the fact that the disciples, especially Peter, were people like us, who battled with human frailties that only Jesus could help them overcome. He was able to teach and show them, by example, the ways of God.

• Show that there's a little bit of Judas in all of us. Also, to ask the questions ... Did Judas betray Jesus solely for money? Or, was Jesus who or what Judas wanted him to be?

• Dispel the belief that the Jews, as a nation, or the Romans put Jesus on the cross, rather, it was a vile spirit of religiosity that ran rampant among the Sanhedrin, Pharisees and Seduces, Scribes and Elders. Would that same spirit put Jesus on the cross today?

• Make it clear that nothing on this earth took Jesus's life...rather, He gave His own life as a sacrifice for the sins of "all" mankind. Only by accepting Jesus Christ as our Lord and Savior will our sins be forgiven and will we receive salvation.

• Let Jesus mold us and shape us into a vessel He can use to take His light wherever darkness dwells.

The Judas Project was created to be a "tool" to be "used" to carry the important message of God's Love to the people of all nations: **"Love is the ultimate power" It is the only weapon with which sin can be driven out, and the only light that can overcome darkness."** It's this message and the reality of God's love, friendship and forgiveness that has made "The Judas Project" the most successful independent theatrical release, dealing with this segment of the life of Jesus Christ, of all time. The commercial success of the motion picture combined with the tremendous spiritual hunger around the world is currently taking "The Judas Project" to all corners of the earth.

It is Emi's and my sincere prayer that God will use the "Interactive Video Study Guide", together with the Video, to bring you into a closer relationship with Him and a deeper understanding of His love for you; and, to encourage you to discover more of God by reading His Word daily.

TABLE OF CONTENTS

JESSE, JUDAS & PETER

AND

OTHER MAIN CHARACTERS

JESSE:

It may surprise some to know that Jesus comes from the root and stem of Jesse. *(Read Matt. 1:1-25)* Also, Jesse means Jehovah exists ... and is another name for Jesus.

> *Isa. 11:1-2   Then a shoot will spring from the stem of Jesse, And a branch from his roots will bear fruit. And the Spirit of the LORD will rest on Him, The spirit of wisdom and understanding, The spirit of counsel and strength, The spirit of knowledge and the fear of the LORD.*

> *Isa. 11:10   Then it will come about in that day That the nations will resort to the root of Jesse, Who will stand as a signal for the peoples; And His resting place will be glorious.*

Most people have their own concept and opinion of God. In most cases, a father is a childs first impression of God; therefore, people view God the way they view their father. If God has never been presented as a God of love, but One who punishes and One to fear, etc., it's reasonable to believe that His Son Jesus is viewed in the same light.

The name Jesse doesn't bring to mind any image at all, and people are more readily open to form an opinion based on a new and fresh look at what this character has to say. He isn't a drawing or a statue without a heart; rather, He is reachable and touchable and most definitely a very real and loving reflection of His Father.

RESULT:

The portrayal of the character of Jesse has helped people realize that Jesus is real. You can touch Him, talk to Him, laugh with Him, feel His heart, His love, forgiveness and accept His healing touch.

His eyes and knowing look disarms even the hardest of hearts. As a result people all over the world, of all ages, are coming to know and accept Jesus Christ as their personal Lord and Savior.   Many have rededicated their lives and others have been taken to a deeper faith walk.

PETER:

Peter represents the disciple Peter. He was a rugged, imperfect, hard working fisherman who was considered to be one of the best at his trade.

Peter wasn't always a "rock" and like us battled with human failures. At times he fell asleep when Jesus prayed. Once out of fear, he denied knowing who Jesus was. Still, he had a heart ... a heart totally sold out to the things of God.

Although his character is a giant of a man, he's missing a left hand. Why? so we wouldn't consider him as perfect; and hopefully, we would learn to look past a handicap and see Peter as a whole and unique individual ... the way God sees him ... the way He sees all of us ...   even through the handicap in our own hearts.

Peter could have been anyone of us standing on the beach early in the morning... broken hearted, ashamed and in desperate need of forgiveness for turning his back not only on the Son of God... but the best friend he ever had.

It was in that moment of need that he reached down deep into his heart, the very dwelling place of Christ, and asked for forgiveness. It was then that he heard a voice behind him, "<u>Do you love me?</u>"

As Peter turned around he was face to face with a resurrected Christ... a friend with outstretched arms and forgiveness in His embrace. Sometimes like Peter we all need that special touch ... a simple hug that says more than words could ever express.

RESULT:

The portrayal of Peter touched people, of all ages. Many have not noticed he was missing a hand or that he didn't say a whole lot ...they just fell in love with the character of Peter. For many, the hug at the end said it all. Still for others, it was also the realization that we shouldn't make spiritual decisions based on what we see or what present circumstances dictate; rather, on what we can't see or touch .... "faith".

Members of various societies for the Handicapped were thankful that Peter was missing a hand. It helped them identify with Peter and to realize that Jesus sees them, as a whole and unique individual with much to contribute.

JUDAS:

Judas represents the disciple Judas. Judas was considered to be a Zealot and like most all Jewish Nationalists of that day, wanted to overthrow the Roman Empire. Jesus represented a new kind of power he'd never known. Could he have wanted Jesus to use His power to overthrow the Roman Empire? Could he have tried to force Jesus to do just that by betraying him? Remember, Judas had the ability to heal others (there were 12 disciples and they went out in pairs to heal the sick, etc.). When Judas betrayed Jesus, did he believe that Jesus could be killed? When Judas realized that Jesus had been condemned, he was so filled with remorse, that he took his own life. The biggest question remains ... why didn't he ask Jesus to forgive him?

RESULT:

Judas is a character we all, most likely, can identify with. People took a long hard look within themselves and wondered if they too could possibly fall into the same trap. As a result, a lot of people rededicated their lives.

PONEROUS:

Ponerous represents the spirit of religiosity, division, confusion and pride found not only in Caiaphas, the Sanhedrin, the Pharisees and the Seduces, but with the Scribes and Elders as well. Within that spirit is the lack of love and forgiveness that's presently on a rampage throughout the world even as it was some 2,000 years ago. Ponerous also represents a person so bound up by the traditions of man and super spirituality that he doesn't recognize the very person God sent ... not to abolish, but to fulfill the law. Instead of embracing Jesse, Ponerous sought to put him to death.

RESULT:

Ponerous hits extremely close to home for some. He was one who chose to speak for God so that the people would follow him and "his church". His character answered many questions as to who killed Jesus and how it could have happened. People found it easier to understand the principalities that Jesus fought against . What happened to Ponerous in the Temple is exactly what God said would eventually happen to his kind. It also brought out the realization that just because someone claims to speak for God doesn't mean he or she truly knows Him.

CUNNINGHAM:

The character of Cunningham represents the world leader, (modern day Rome) and the embodiment of Caesar, Pilot and Herod ... all rolled into the very spirit that caused him to seek to control the very thing that already controlled him ..."Power". Why with all his power did Cunningham not want to kill Jesse? Who did he turn Jesse over to?

RESULT:

It wasn't Cunningham that ordered Jesse's death... it was Ponerous. The character of Cunningham made it easy for most people to recognize the fact of how easily pride, power, or the love of money can shut out humility ... blinding us to the truth and recognition of Jesus.

JACKSON:

Jackson's character simply represents a different kind of thief... one who takes your life. Even though he is portrayed as a hit man... who kills people for a living, he also recognized who Jesse was. That's why, as he himself hung from the cross dying, he asked to go with Jesse. Why do you think Jesse said; "This day you will be with me in paradise?" Jesse knew Jackson's heart.

RESULT:

It was astonishing to find out how many people felt that God (Jesus) knows your heart and whether or not you are sincere. His character hit a lot of people square in the heart and they felt if Jesus could forgive him, He could also forgive them. Again, lives were rededicated, and changed.

BROTHER DeCARMO:

Brother DeCarmo's character represents another kind of thief and robber. He is one who can rob you of your soul. His character is that of a Shepherd who takes an oath to lay down his life for his sheep, but when the wolves come, he runs away and leaves them defenseless. He is one who really doesn't know Jesus and one who would never recognize Him... even if he was dying on the cross beside Him.

RESULT:

Some people couldn't figure out why he was on the cross. Others, especially Christians, were hit hard by the analogy. It woke up a lot of people .

How To Use
and
Co-Ordinate
The Interactive Study Guide
with
The Video

HOW TO USE
"THE INTERACTIVE VIDEO STUDY GUIDE"

You will find that the "Interactive Video Study Guide" covers a tremendous amount of territory in regard to Jesus, the disciples, their relationship to each other and how it relates to and affects us individually. It is not intended to answer every question; rather, to address some of the issues that are pertinent to our salvation and spiritual well being. Although we have included and written out scripture references, it is most important that you also read them in your own Bible. It is our desire that you will search further into God's Word on your own.

The "Interactive Video Study Guide" can be used by itself; however, using the Interactive Video Study Guide along with the Video and Bible will greatly enhance the overall impact of its message. They are designed to work together "interactively" much like Paul and Apollos. One plants and the other waters but it's God's Word (Bible) that brings forth the increase.

> *1Cor. 3:5-6 What then is Apollos? And what is Paul? Servants through whom you believed, even as the Lord gave {opportunity} to each one. I (Paul) planted, Apollos watered, but <u>God was causing the growth.</u>*

The "Interactive Video Study Guide" is broken down into 26 individual scenes. Each scene is made up of two parts: the "Screenplay Dialogue Script" and its corresponding "Study Scene". It can be used by any family and/or study group, as well as, an individual.

Playing the motion picture "Sound Track" is an excellent way to get into the mood of the study, as a lot of the film's message is contained in the lyrics of the songs.

HOW TO CO-ORDINATE
"THE INTERACTIVE VIDEO STUDY GUIDE"
WITH THE VIDEO

Start the video at the beginning of the movie and follow along with the Dialogue Script. When you reach the end of the scene, put the VCR on "Pause" (if you wish to study more than one scene); or "Stop" if you wish to study only that one scene and continue on at a later date.

When you are ready to proceed to the next scene, start the Video at the point where you previously "Paused" or "Stopped".

We encourage everyone to discuss each scene openly and frankly, as varied opinions can lead to greater depth and under-standing. **<u>Always use the Bible as the final authority on any and all issues</u>**.

Dialogue Continuity Script

and

Study Scenes

"THE JUDAS PROJECT"   DIALOGUE SCRIPT

EXT. BEACH. NIGHT: (SCENE 1)

	(Helicopter lands on beach. Spotlight shines on JESSE being surrounded by armed men. Trucks pull up, more helicopters land circling JESSE. JUDAS walks toward JESSE. They look at each other.)
JUDAS:	WHY??!!
GRAPHIC OVER	Two Years Earlier

EXT. BEACH. NIGHT:

	(Sirens, flashing lights. Squad car pull up)
COAST GUARD:	(OS) Rescue, this is Coast Guard Rescue. Could you shine your search light out a little bit ahead of our bow please?
	(COP adjusts light.)
	(CONT'D) Thank you, Mobile Rescue.... moving a few yards north... still looking... Coast Guard standing by.
	(Police car drives on past news crew.)
NEWSMAN:	(OS) And ... go.
JUDITH CHILDS:	We're here at the scene where a little more than three hours have passed since the young man was apparently

EXT. BEACH. NIGHT: (CONTINUED)

J. CHILDS (CONT'D): swept from the point...

> (MOTHER walks up.)

> (OS) by the tremendous undercurrent while fishing. Local officials here don't seem to be offering any hope for the possibility that the young man may still be alive. For WNTW, this is Judith Childs.

> (Sirens, booming sounds of water being dragged. JUDAS watches.)

COAST GUARD: (VO) Stand by

> (Men with flashlights run towards camera, run back towards water. JUDAS walks toward shore.)

CROWD: Watch out! Over here! There he is! Stay away from the water! Etc.

> (POLICEMAN and EMT WOMAN pull DROWNED BOY from water.)

EMT WOMAN: Lift, his feet! Get the water out of his waders! Etc.

EMT MAN: I'm trying ... I'm trying

> (RESCUE WORKER holds back crowd.)

EXT. BEACH. NIGHT: (CONTINUED)

RESCUE WORKER: Stay back please.

                   (Other RESCUE WORKERS surround
                   BOY.)

RESCUE WORKERS: Is he alive? Easy, easy. Get him on the
                   stretcher. He's gone. He's gone. Etc.

                   (MOTHER comes through crowd, sees
                   BOY.)

POLICEMAN: (VO) Let her through. Make room,
                   please. Stand back.

CROWD: Set him down. Let her through, etc.

                   (CROWD quiets. Sheet is pulled back
                   from BOY's face.)

MOTHER: (Crying) Oh, God. How could you kill
                   my son? (OS) How could you kill my
                   son?! HOW COULD YOU? (Cries.)

                   (JESSE places his hand on BOY's heart.
                   BOY coughs and sits up.)

MOTHER: Oh, my God. Oh, my God. Oh, my God.

                   (CROWD murmurs.)

BOY: The light ... it's beautiful!

MOTHER: (OS) Oh, baby

BOY: It's Beautiful.

EXT. BEACH. NIGHT: (CONTINUED)

MOTHER: (OS) Oh, baby.

                        (JESSE walks through crowd.)

MOTHER: Oh, God! .... you're alive.

                        (MOTHER hugs BOY)

JUDITH CHILDS: Coming in three, two, one. Miracle or
                        not, the young man who was dead .....
                        isn't. And the man identified as "JESSE,"
                        who apparently is responsible for what-
                        ever happened here tonight, left as he
                        arrived, suddenly. And what was sure
                        tragedy just a moment ago is now a story
                        with a happy ending that is sure to raise a
                        lot of questions within each and every one
                        of us. As for the answers, well that de-
                        pends on what, or in whom, we believe.

                        (OPENING TITLE)

THE JUDAS PROJECT

JBE

STUDY SCENE:
NO. 1

In this scene, the boy's death was obviously an accident due to his carelessness. He simply walked out to far and deep into the water. The current swept him off his feet, filling his waders with water, and pulled him under. It was a very unfortunate choice that the boy made, and because of it, suffered the consequences.

1. Why then was the boy's mother accusing God of killing her son? How often does God get blamed for the death of loved ones, as if He takes pleasure in it?

> *Ezek. 18:32 "For I have no pleasure in the death of anyone who dies," declares the Lord GOD.*
>
> *Eccl. 3:1-8 There is an appointed time for every-thing. And there is a time for every event under heaven; A time to give birth, and a time to die; A time to plant, and a time to uproot what is planted. A time to kill, and a time to heal; A time to tear down, and a time to build up. A time to weep, and a time to laugh; A time to mourn, and a time to dance. A time to throw stones, and a time to gather stones; A time to embrace, and a time to shun embracing. A time to search, and a time to give up as lost; A time to keep, and a time to throw away. A time to tear apart, and a time to sew together; A time to be silent, and a time to speak. A time to love, and a time to hate; A time for war, and a time for peace.*

2. What do you think was behind the look that Jesse gave the boy's mother?

A. Was it one of compassion and understanding? Or;

B. One of condemnation?

> *Luke 7:13 When the Lord saw her, He had*
> *compassion for her..*

3. When the boy was raised from the dead, why did he say, "the light ... it's beautiful, it's beautiful" although his eyes were still closed?

A. Was it the flashing of the cameras? Or;

B. Perhaps the radiance of God's Glory?

> *Luke 7:15 The dead man sat up and began to speak,*
> *and Jesus gave him to his mother.*
>
> *Matt. 17:2 .... and His face shone like the sun.*
>
> *1 John 1:5 .... God is light and in Him there is no*
> *darkness at all.*

4. When the mother saw her son raised from the dead, did she take the time to thank God for restoring her son's life?

A. Shouldn't we take the time to thank God in all things ... including adversity?

> *Eph. 5:20 ... giving thanks to God the Father at all*
> *times and for everything in the name of our Lord*
> *Jesus Christ.*
>
> *Luke 17:15-16 Then one of them, when he saw that*
> *he was healed, turned back, praising God with a loud*
> *voice. He prostrated himself at Jesus' feet and*
> *thanked Him....*

5. Even though the reporter witnessed a miracle, why was she "on the fence" by not reporting it as a miracle of God?

    A. Afraid of possible ridicule/peer pressure? Or;

    B. Afraid to believe what she actually witnessed?

> *2 Cor. 4:4 In their case the god of this world has blinded the minds of the unbelievers, to keep them from seeing the light of the gospel of the glory of Christ, who is the image of God.*

Do we always acknowledge ... give God the glory for miracles, big or small, that He performs in our lives? Or like the reporter do we refuse to believe, and simply attribute them to good fortune, luck .... or maybe the by-product of the right circumstances coming together?

Our God is a compassionate God. In our daily routine we may not always realize this, yet it is through our greatest times of trial or loss, that we draw strength from Him and cling to Him. During such times, Jesus becomes a quiet servant, ministering life and peace to us.

ADDITIONAL BIBLICAL REFERENCES:
(The dead are brought back to life.)

Read Matt. 9:24-25
Read Mark 5:35-42
Read Luke 8:51-55
Read John 11:38-44

NOTES

EXT. BEACH. DAY: (SCENE 2 & 3)

(JUDAS walks along beach toward gathering of people.)

JESSE: (OS) Don't worry about the way others live. Perfect yourselves first, with the strength that I give you. And don't be afraid ... the rescuer comes to a drowning man, not a great swimmer. It would be better that some were made blind in order that they would see. Love is a powerful key. It overcomes hate ...

(IN FRAME) Just as light over comes darkness.

(JESSE touches BLIND MAN.)

JESSE: Receive the light!

(BLIND MAN "sees", looks at his WIFE for the first time.)

BLIND MAN: You're more beautiful than I ever imagined!

(BLIND MAN and WIFE embrace ... WIFE begins to cry)

(JUDAS watches JESSE walk through crowd toward MAN ON CRUTCHES.)

JESSE: (OS) I can't teach a man to walk who's trusting in a crutch.

EXT. BEACH. DAY (CONT'D)

JESSE (CONT'D):   (IN FRAME) Don't limit me ... my power has no limits.

      (OS) Do you have faith?

MAN ON CRUTCHES: I've always had faith.

JESSE: It's good to have faith ... (OS) but it's of little use to you ...

      (IN FRAME) unless you believe in that faith.

      (MAN begins to hand over crutches.)

MAN ON CRUTCHES: No...

      (JESSE looks the MAN ON CRUTCHES straight in the eyes)

JESSE: Believe ... and go your way.

      (MAN ON CRUTCHES walks over and embraces friend.)

MAN ON CRUTCHES: (OS) They work .... look Bill ... they really work!

      (MAN ON CRUTCHES turns .. walks toward JESSE.

JESSE: embraces him in a bear hug.... pats him on the back .... then turns to the crowd)

LADY IN CROWD: (VO) I want to believe...

EXT. BEACH. DAY   (CONT'D):

                         (JESSE turns and looks toward
                         CROWD)

JESSE: No life is small to God. All life has
                         value ... but it's the quality of life ...
                         that determines the value.

LADY IN CROWD: (OS) Touch me, too.

                         (JESSE touches her, as he walks
                         through CROWD toward JUDAS)

JESSE: Just as the physician heals the sick,
                         and not the healthy, so it is that I
                         have come into the world to save the
                         lost ... that through me you would
                         have eternal life ... and if you
                         believe...

                         (To JUDAS as JESSE places his hand
                         on JUDAS' SHOULDER)

JESSE: (OS) If you believe, you will never be
                         lonely.

                         (JUDAS.. frightened .. backs away, runs
                         toward van, drives off.)

STUDY SCENE
NO: 2 & 3

In this scene, Judas, attracted by a crowd gathered around Jesse, joins in... yet stands off by himself. As it was his custom, Jesse was not only teaching but also healing all those in need. There are many kinds of healing. Healing the attitudes of our heart often seems to take the longest.

Nothing is hidden from God as He knows our innermost thoughts. He was present while we were knitted together in our mother's womb. His eyes have seen our unformed substance and all the days, ordained for us, are written in His book. He knows all of our ways and desires for us to grow and be perfected by His Word.

1. Jesse makes the following statements.

    A. "Don't worry about the way others live. Perfect your-selves first, with the strength that I give you."

        Ps. 139:23-24 Search me, O God, and know my heart; Try me and know my anxious thoughts; And see if there be any hurtful way in me, And lead me in the everlasting way.

        Ps. 143:10   Teach me to do Thy will, For Thou art my God; Let Thy good Spirit lead me on level ground.

        Phil. 2:3-5   Do nothing from selfishness or empty conceit, but with humility of mind let each of you regard one another as more important than himself; do not {merely} look out for your own personal int-erests, but also for the interests of others.   Have this attitude in yourselves which was also in Christ Jesus,

NOTE: When we become to concerned about the way others live, we also become critical or faultfinding and start pointing a finger at each other. If we take the time to look at our hand while our finger is pointed toward others we also see, "much to our sorrow", not one... but three fingers pointing back at us.

> *Luke 6:41-42* **"And why do you look at the speck that is in your brother's eye, but do not notice the log that is in your own eye? Or, how can you say to your brother, 'Brother, let me take out the speck that is in your eye,' when you yourself do not see the log that is in your own eye? You hypocrite, first take the log out of your own eye, and then you will see clearly to take out the speck that is in your brother's eye."**

> *Matt. 7:12* **"Therefore, however you want people to treat you, so treat them, for this is the Law and the Prophets."**

Fear has a paralyzing affect on anyone who yields to it. He goes on ... saying:

B. "Don't be afraid ...the rescuer comes to a drowning man not a great swimmer."

> *Matt. 14:30-31 .... he became frightened, and beginning to sink, he cried out, "Lord, save me!" Jesus immediately reached out His hand and caught him...*

> *Ps. 56:3 When I am afraid, I will put my trust in Thee.*

> *Phil. 4:6-7 Be anxious for nothing, but in everything by prayer and supplication with thanksgiving let your requests be made known to God. And the*

> *peace of God, which surpasses all comprehension,*
> *shall guard your hearts and your minds in Christ*
> *Jesus.*

C. "It would be better that some were made blind in order that they would see."

> *John 9:39-41 Jesus said,* ***"I came into this world***
> ***for judgement so that those who do not see may***
> ***see, and those who do see may become blind."*** *Some*
> *of the Pharisees near Him heard this and said to*
> *Him, "Surely we are not blind, are we?" Jesus said*
> *to them,* ***"If you were blind, you would not have***
> ***sin. But now that you say, 'We see', your sin***
> ***remains."***

D. "Love is a powerful key ... it overcomes hate just as light overcomes darkness."

> *Prov. 10:12 Hatred stirs up strife, but love covers*
> *all transgressions.*

> *John 1:4-5 In Him was life, and the life was the*
> *light of all people. The light shines in the*
> *darkness, and the darkness did not overcome it.*

E. "Receive the Light!"

> *Mark 8:25 Then Jesus laid his hands on his eyes*
> *again; and he looked intently and his sight was*
> *restored, and he saw everything clearly.*

We are blind and void of all understanding until, through His Love, God gives us the "light" to truly see and understand. Only then can we see and exclaim like the blind man (who is seeing his wife for the first time) "You're more beautiful than I'd ever imagined."

F. "I can't teach a man to walk who's trusting in a crutch. Don't limit me ... my power has no limits".

> *Num. 11:23   The LORD said to Moses, "Is the LORD's power limited? Now you shall see whether My word will come true for you or not."*

> *Luke 1:37   For nothing will be impossible with God.*

For many of us, acting on faith is like being in unchartered waters ... without maps or instruments to depend on to get to where we want to be. It is much like a little child that is just learning to walk and sees the outstretched arms of its father and takes that first step toward him. Notice that it requires two things ... believing and action.

G. "It's good to have faith, but it's of little use to you ... unless you <u>believe</u> in that faith."

> *Heb . 11:6   And without faith it is impossible to please God, for whoever would approach Him <u>must believe</u> that He exists and that He rewards those who seek Him.*

> *Gal. 3:22   But the scripture has imprisoned all things under the power of sin, so that what was promised through faith in Jesus Christ might be given to those who believe.*

> *Mark 2:11-12   **"I say to you, rise, take up your pallet and go home."** And he rose and immediately took up the pallet and went out in the sight of all; so that they were all amazed and were glorifying God.*

> *Mark 5:36   **"Do not be afraid {any} {longer,} only believe."***

> *1Cor. 2:5   that your faith should not rest on the*
> *wisdom of men, but on the power of God.*

H. "No life is small to God. All life has value ... but, it's
the quality of life that determines the value."

> *Rev. 4:11   You are worthy, our Lord and God, to*
> *receive glory and honor and power, for You created*
> *all things, and by Your will they existed and were*
> *created.*

> *Matt. 6:26   **"Look at the birds of the air, that they***
> ***do not sow, neither do they reap, nor gather into***
> ***barns, and {yet} your heavenly Father feeds them.***
> ***Are you not worth much more than they?"***

> *Matt. 6:33   **"But seek first His kingdom and His***
> ***righteousness;"***

> *Matt. 6:19-21   **"Do not lay up for yourselves trea-***
> ***sures upon earth, where moth and rust destroy, and***
> ***where thieves break in and steal.   But lay up for***
> ***yourselves treasures in heaven, where neither moth***
> ***nor rust destroys, and where thieves do not break***
> ***in or steal;   for where your treasure is, there will***
> ***your heart be also."***

> *Heb . 13:7   Remember your leaders, those who*
> *spoke the word of God to you; consider the*
> *outcome of their way of life, and imitate their*
> *faith.*

I. "Just as the physician heals the sick, and not the healthy,
so it is that I have come into the world to save   the lost
that through me you would have eternal life. And, if you
believe you'll never be lonely."

> *Matt. 9:12   ...But when He heard this, He said,*

"Those who are well have no need of a physician, but those who are sick."

John 12:47 "I do not judge anyone who hears my words and does not keep them, for I came not to judge the world, but to save the world."

John 6:40 "This is indeed the will of my Father, that all who see the Son and believe in Him may have eternal life; and I will raise them up on the last day."

John 3:16 "For God so loved the world that He gave His only Son, so that everyone who believes in Him may not perish but may have eternal life."

Heb . 13:5 Keep your lives free from the love of money, and be content with what you have; for He has said, "I will never leave you or forsake you."

2. Why do you think Judas ran away?

    A. Was he afraid? Or;

    B. Could it have been that his heart and mind were at war?

Matt. 13:15 "For this people's heart has grown dull, and their ears are hard of hearing, and they have shut their eyes; so that they might not look with their eyes, and listen with their ears, and understand with their heart and turn and I would heal them."

ADDITIONAL BIBLICAL REFERENCES:
(On various healings performed by Jesus)

Matthew 8:5-13   *Mark 10:46-52*
Matt. 9:1-8   *Luke 7:1-10*
Matt. 20:29-34   *Luke 14:2-4*
Mark 3:1-5   *Luke 18:35-43*
Mark 8:22-25

NOTES

INT. RESTAURANT. NIGHT: (SCENE 4 & 5)

	(MAN turns on jukebox.)
JUDAS:	(OS) I may be from New York ...
	(IN FRAME) but you don't expect me to believe a dead guy just gets up and walks away. I mean, you're good... but, you're not that good.
	(OS) Only God Almighty Himself in the flesh could pull that off
	(IN FRAME) and I don't think He's down here on vacation ... fishing... do you?
JESSE:	Why do you choose to disbelieve what you already believe in your heart is true?
JUDAS:	Everything and everyone has a price. What's yours?
JESSE:	You couldn't pay it. It's a gift, freely given.
JUDAS:	(OS) Let's say for arguments sake,
	(IN FRAME) that I believe this kid was dead and you brought him back to life. That means you possess a power unlike anyone on this earth and that, in itself, would excite me. But, it would also mean that you're the Son of God, the "Anointed One" the world has been waiting for since the beginning

INT. RESTAURANT. NIGHT: (CONT'D):

JUDAS (CONT'D):   of time. Now that, that would frighten me. And I choose to disbelieve, as you put it, because I find it hard to believe that God would come down, pick somebody up from the dead and then just walk away... see, which is exactly what you did. Now, if it was real, and the news media certainly thinks it was, why don't you go on television? Why don't you tell the world who you are? Why don't you use the   power you supposedly have?

JESSE: To do what?

JUDAS: Oh, I don't know. Take over the world.

JESSE: (OS) Then what?

JUDAS: Force it to be what you created it to be.

JESSE: (OS) The world wasn't created out of force but out of love.

    (IN FRAME) and God is love. Therefore, He truly gives and requires love that is unconditional,

    (OS) It can't be bought or forced.

JUDAS: Earlier, I heard you speak about love being a powerful key to overcome hate, I've never known that kind, or any other kind of love. See, I grew up

INT. RESTAURANT. NIGHT: (CONT'D):

JUDAS (CONT'D):   in a city that is full of hate and fear ... and the only thing that anybody ever understood was power.

(OS) Do you think it's different

(IN FRAME) throughout America, or the rest of the world? The money I deal with every day may say, "In God We Trust," but we don't. We really trust the power and the security money can buy. You see the battles on this earth are fought for power, not for love.

(OS) So, the day you convince me that love is stronger than power, I'll start believing all this stuff you're dishing out to everybody.

JESSE: Love is... the ultimate power. It's the only weapon with which sin can be driven out. To love someone you must truly know and understand that individual.

(OS) To accomplish much, you must first be much

(IN FRAME) and then if you truly wish to conquer, you must trust in God

(OS) because only He will give you

(IN FRAME) the only safety, security and guidance that you'll ever know.

INT. RESTAURANT. NIGHT: (CONT'D):

JUDAS: I am not insecure, alright? I know who I am. I know where I am going. You trust in God. I'll believe in me. And as for your remark to me earlier today, I'd rather believe in me than you. And you know what? I'm not lonely.

JESSE: Is that why you left?

JUDAS: You wanna know why I left. Because I don't understand all of this stuff I see going on in here. And how would you like it if I am the one performing miracles, I walk up to you and I say, "I have come into the world to save the lost ... through me you can have eternal life ... and if you believe in me, you'll never be lonely again." I'm sorry! ... I can't believe in someone or something I don't understand.

(OS) I don't even know you.

JESSE: (OS) You will. You will.

STUDY SCENE
NO: 4 & 5

In this scene, we are introduced to the humanity of Judas and the battles going on in his heart and mind. Like many of us Judas was also influenced by his environment and had enormous difficulty trusting. He knew much about hatred and arguing. Seeing miracles take place before his eyes, wasn't something he was eager to accept or believe.

1. Why did Judas have difficulty believing the miracles that were taking place right in front of his eyes?

> *1Cor. 2:14 Those who are unspiritual do not receive the gifts of God's Spirit, for they are foolishness to them, and they are unable to understand them because they are spiritually discerned.*

2. How could Jesse say to Judas "Why do you choose to disbelieve what you already believe in your heart is true?"

> *Ps. 44:21 ...would not God discover this? For He knows the secrets of the heart.*

3. When Judas said to Jesse, "everything and everyone has a price what's yours?", what did Jesse mean by "You couldn't pay it ... It's a gift freely given?

> *Mark 10:45* **"For the Son of Man came not to be served but to serve, and <u>to give His life</u> a ransom for many."**
>
> *Rom. 6:23 For the wages of sin is death, but the free gift of God is eternal life in Christ Jesus our Lord.*

4. What did Judas mean when he said; "Why don't you go on TV? Why don't you tell the world who you are?"

> John 7:4   *For no one who wants to be widely known acts in secret. If you do these things, show yourself to the world.*

5.   If Judas sees Jesse as one to overthrow the worldly power structure ... right all the wrongs .... force the world to be what he (Jesse, the Son of God) created it to be:

   A. Why did Jesse say, "And then what?"

> Luke 9:55-56 ...**"You do not know what spirit you are of; For the Son of Man did not come to destroy man's life, but to save them."**
>
> Mark 8:36   **"For what will it profit them to gain the whole world and forfeit their life?"**
>
> Matt. 10:34-39   **"Do not think that I have come to bring peace to the earth; I have not come to bring peace, but a sword.   For I have come to set a man against his father, and a daughter against her mother, and a daughter-in-law against her mother-in-law;   and one's foes will be members of one's own household. Whoever loves father or mother more than me is not worthy of me; and whoever loves son or daughter more than me is not worthy of me;   and whoever does not take up the cross and follow me is not worthy of me. Those who find their life will lose it, and those who lose their life for my sake will find it.**

   B Jesse states: "The world wasn't created out of force but out of love ... and God is love," How could he make that statement?

John 10:30 **"The Father and I are one."**

1John 4:8 *Whoever does not love, does not know God, for God is love.*

C. Why did Jesse say, "God requires love that is unconditional ... it can't be bought or forced?"

Mark 12:30 *Jesus answered,* **"you shall love the Lord your God with all your heart, and with all your soul, and with all your mind, and with all your strength.'**

Prov. 8:17 *I love those who love Me; and those who diligently seek Me will find Me.*

Matt. 7:7-8 **"Ask, and it shall be given to you; seek, and you shall find; knock, and it shall be opened to you. For everyone who asks receives, and he who seeks finds, and to him who knocks it shall be opened."**

6. What happens to us if, rather than believing in God, we trust in the power and security money can buy?

Matt. 6:24 **"No one can serve two masters; for either he will hate the one and love the other, or he will hold to one and despise the other. You cannot serve God and wealth."**

Matt. 6:19-21 **"Do not lay up for yourselves treasures upon earth, where moth and rust destroy, and where thieves break in and steal. But lay up for yourselves treasures in heaven, where neither moth nor rust destroy, and where thieves do not break in or steal; For where your treasure is, there will your heart be also."**

7. What is the price of fighting battles on this earth for power... instead of love?

> *Matt. 6:26* **"For what will a man be profited, if he gains the whole world, and forfeits his soul? Or what will a man give in exchange for his soul?**
>
> *Rom. 12:18*   *If it is possible, so far as it depends on you, live in peace with all men..*

8. When Judas asked Jesse to convince him that love was stronger than power, what was Jesse's response?

"Love is the ultimate power. It's the only weapon with which sin can be driven out. To love someone, you must truly know and understand that individual. To acomplish much, you must first be much, then If you truly wish to conquer you must trust in God, because only He will give you the only safety, security and guidance that you'll ever know."

> *1Cor. 13:13*   *And now faith, hope, and love abide, these three; <u>and the greatest of these is love</u>.*
>
> *Lam. 3:22*   *The steadfast love of the LORD never ceases, His mercies never come to an end;*
>
> *Prov. 10:12*   *Hatred stirs up strife, but love covers all sin.*
>
> *1John 4:16*   *God is love, and the one who abides in love abides in God, and God abides in him.*
>
> *Ps. 118:8*   *It is better to take refuge in the Lord than to trust in man.*

Ps. 4:8   In peace I will both lie down and sleep, for Thou alone, O LORD, dost make me to dwell in safety.

Hebr. 13:5   Keep your lives free from the love of money, and be content with what you have; for He has said, "I will never leave you or forsake you."

Rom. 8:38-39   For I am convinced that neither death, nor life, nor angels, nor principalities, nor things present, nor things to come, nor powers, nor height, nor death, nor any other created thing, shall be able to separate us from the love of God, which is in Christ Jesus our Lord.

9.   Judas said he'd rather trust and believe in himself, rather than Jesse;

     A. What is the price tag of self pride and self sufficiency?

         Prov. 28:26   He who trusts in his own heart is a fool, but he who walks wisely will be delivered.

         Prov. 9:23   A man's pride will bring him low, but a humble spirit will obtain honor.

         Prov. 11:28   He who trusts in his riches will fall. ..

10.   How is it possible to believe or trust in someone or something we don't understand?

     A. Trust:

         Prov. 3:5   <u>Trust</u> in the Lord with all your heart, and do not lean on your own understanding.

B. Faith:

> *Rom. 1:17   BUT THE RIGHTEOUS {man} SHALL LIVE BY FAITH.*
>
> *Romans 12:3   ... God has allotted to each a measure of <u>faith</u>.*
>
> *Hebr. 11:1   Now <u>faith</u> is the assurance of things hoped for, the conviction of things not seen.*
>
> *Hebr. 11:6   And <u>without faith</u> it is impossible to please God, for he who comes to God must believe that He is a rewarder of those who seek Him.*
>
> *2Cor. 5:7   for we walk by faith, not by sight*

Faith based on tradition or habit, is not the same as faith that is built on personal commitment to God and His Word.

NOTES:

EXT. CUNNINGHAM'S HOME. DAY   (SCENE 6 & 7)

(NO DIALOGUE.)

INT. CUNNINGHAM'S HOME. DAY:

>   (CUNNINGHAM watches slides. Snaps his fingers to change each slide.)

CUNNINGHAM: She has forgotten that we are the source of her power.

>   (OS) General Juan Cervantes ... Her replacement Jackson.

JACKSON: Yes, Mr. Cunningham, I understand.

CUNNINGHAM: (OS) Louise Brockton. Possible Supreme Court appointee. I want to know who shares the air she breathes and why... In three days!

JACKSON: Done.

CUNNINGHAM: (OS) How long have we been watching Jesse?

JACKSON: (OS) About two years.

CUNNINGHAM: (OS) Tremendous acceleration in his followers.

>   (IN FRAME) This man could become a world leader. Have you noticed the change in Judas? Look at him! Ha! ... he has an assurance about him I haven't seen before. I understand that look very well. I want you to start a file on that man. That will be all, Jackson.

INT. CUNNINGHAM'S HOME. DAY (CONT'D):

CUNNINGHAM (CONT'D):   Oh, Jackson,

        (OS) get in touch with Asa.

        (IN FRAME) I have a new project for her.

        (CUNNINGHAM pushes intercom)

SECRETARY: (VO) Yes, Mr. Cunningham?

CUNNINGHAM: Send in Ponerous.

SECRETARY: (VO) I'm afraid he's already on his way in.

CUNNINGHAM: Can I ask what sort of mood he's in to-day?

PONEROUS: (OS) Mr. Cunningham.

        (IN FRAME) Why was I not allowed to participate in this meeting? ... and since when do you exclude the voice of the Church?

CUNNINGHAM: Since when does your Church question my authority? Why all this concern about this Jesse character?

PONEROUS: This very persuasive, indignant personality maligns the integrity of this Order. He's obsessed with these miracles which are contrary to the beliefs and completely without the sanction of the Church.

INT. CUNNINGHAM'S HOME. DAY (CONT'D):

PONEROUS (CONT'D):   In other words, Mr. Cunningham, put this to an end before it goes any further.

CUNNINGHAM: Ha! Ponerous, my cunning old friend ...

(OS) both you and your Church are a constant source of irritation to me and the Board.

(IN FRAME) I tolerate it because I would find it most difficult to ... eradicate the beliefs of so many people. However, I... am the authority ...

(OS) and neither I nor the Board will ever be used by you to stop any man who could bring about an insurrection within your Church ...

(IN FRAME) unless, of course it could, ah, affect us adversely ... which, is not the case here, now is it?

PONEROUS: It's obvious you don't understand, much less appreciate, the real peril ... this young Jesse represents.

CUNNINGHAM: I understand that there is a man traveling around this country talking about a new kind of religion. Now, there must be something to it because he's got half the country turned upside down and look at you, he's scaring the hell out of you.

PONEROUS: And you're doing nothing?

INT. CUNNINGHAM'S HOME. DAY (CONT'D):

CUNNINGHAM: Wrong! I'm watching every move he
                 makes. He may prove useful to us.

PONEROUS: You'll never use him. He'll destroy
                 you.

CUNNINGHAM: If he destroys anyone it'll be you ... not
                 me. (Smiling at PONEROUS) I have
                 what he wants.

STUDY SCENE:
NO. 6 & 7

As this scene unfolds Cunningham is established as a man of great world power, and one not afraid to use it. Ponerous, on the other hand, is a man of "religious power" who wields his authority as it best serves his interests. Both relish the positions they hold and try to work together through their irreconcilable differences. All seems tolerable until a young man, Jesse, arrives on the scene like a "fast rising tide"..with his ever increasing followers. Ponerous growing fearful and threatened by Jesse's popularity turns to Cunningham for help ... demanding him to put an end to it.

1. Were the Pharisees, Seduces, Chief Priests, Scribes, Elders, etc. really afraid of the teachings of Jesus and the miracles he was performing.... especially on the Sabbath ... even to the point of putting Him to death?

> *Luke 6:7   The scribes and the Pharisees watched Him to see whether he would heal on the Sabbath, so that they might find an accusation against Him.*

> *Matt. 12:2   When the Pharisees saw it, they said to Him, "Look, your disciples are doing what is not lawful to do on the Sabbath.*

> *Matt. 21:23   When He entered the temple, the chief priests and the elders of the people came to Him as He was teaching, and said, "<u>By what authority are You doing these things, and who gave You this authority?</u>"*

> *Matt. 12:8-14 **"For the Son of Man is Lord of the Sabbath."** And departing from there, He went into their synagogue.   And behold, {there was} a man*

with a withered hand. And they questioned Him, saying, "Is it lawful to heal on the Sabbath?" in order that they might accuse Him. And He said to them, **"What man shall there be among you, who shall have one sheep, and if it falls into a pit on the Sabbath, will he not take hold of it, and lift it out? "Of how much more value then is a man than a sheep! So then, it is lawful to do good on the Sabbath."** *Then He said to the man,* **"Stretch out your hand!"** *And he stretched it out, and it was restored to normal, like the other. But the Pharisees went out, and counseled together against Him, as to how they might destroy Him.*

Mark 11:18 And when the chief priests and the scribes heard it, they kept looking for a way to kill Him; <u>for they were afraid of Him</u>, because the whole crowd was spellbound by His teaching.

2.   How did Jesus recognize Caesar's authority, while at the same time, evade the trap being set for Him by the Pharisees?

Matt. 22:15-21 Then the Pharisees went and counseled together how they might trap Him in what He said. And they sent their disciples to Him along with the Herodians, saying, 'Teacher, we know that You are truthful and teach the way of God in truth, and defer to no one; for You are not partial to any. Tell us therefore, what do You think? Is it lawful to give a poll tax to Caesar, or not?' But Jesus perceived their malice, and said, **'Why are you testing Me, you hypocrites? Show me the coin used for the poll tax'.** *And they brought Him a denarius. And He said to them,* **"Whose likeness and inscription is this?'** *They said to Him, 'Caesars.' Then He said to them,* **"Then render to Caesar the things that are Caesars; and to God the things that are Gods."**

3. Like the Pharisees, Ponerous is only interested in his own purpose and personal gain.

> *Luke 7:30   But the Pharisees and the lawyers   re-jected God's purpose for themselves, not having been baptized by John.*

> *Jude 4   For certain persons have crept in un-noticed, those who were long beforehand marked out for this condemnation, ungodly persons who turn the grace of our God into licentiousness and deny our only Master and Lord, Jesus Christ.*

> *Jude 19   These are the ones who cause divisions, worldly-minded, devoid of the Spirit.*

4.   Whenever possible the Pharisees and Sadducees tested Jesus looking for signs from heaven and, while looking, never recognized the obvious signs of the times.

> *Matt. 16:1-4   And the Pharisees and Sadducees came up, and testing Him asked Him to show them a sign from heaven. But He answered and said to them, **"When it is evening, you say, ' {It will be} fair weather, for the sky is red.' "And in the morning, {'There will be} a storm today, for the sky is red and threatening.' Do you know how to discern the appearance of the sky, but cannot {discern} the signs of the times?   "An evil and adulterous generation seeks after a sign; and a sign will not be given it, except the sign of Jonah."** And He left them, and went away.*

5. The Pharisees and Sadducees were more interested in the traditions of man than God's commandments... and like Ponerous, were easily offended by the truth.

Matt. 15:1-14   Then some Pharisees and scribes came to Jesus from Jerusalem, saying,   "Why do Your disciples transgress the tradition of the elders? For they do not wash their hands when they eat bread."   And He answered and said to them, **"And why do you yourselves transgress the commandment of God for the sake of your tradition?   "For God said, 'HONOR YOUR FATHER AND MOTHER,' and, 'HE WHO SPEAKS EVIL OF FATHER OR MOTHER, LET HIM BE PUT TO DEATH.' "But you say, 'Whoever shall say to {his} father or mother,   Anything of mine you might have been helped by has been given {to God,} he is not to honor his father or his mother.' And {thus} you invalidated the word of God for the sake of your tradition."   "You hypocrites, rightly did Isaiah prophesy of you, saying, 'THIS PEOPLE HONORS ME WITH THEIR LIPS, BUT THEIR HEART IS FAR AWAY FROM ME.   BUT IN VAIN DO THEY WORSHIP ME, TEACHING AS DOCTRINES THE PRECEPTS OF MEN.'"** *And after He called the multitude to Him, He said to them,* **"Hear, and understand.   Not what enters into the mouth defiles the man, but what proceeds out of the mouth, this defiles the man."** *Then the disciples came and said to Him, "Do You know that the Pharisees were offended when they heard this statement?"   But He answered and said,* **"Every plant which My heavenly Father did not plant shall be rooted up.   Let them alone; they are blind guides of the blind. And if a blind man guides a blind man, both will fall into a pit."**

6. Ponerous was both; aware of, and threatened by, the growing popularity of Jesse as were the Pharisees and Sadducees in regard to Jesus.

Matt. 15:29-31   And departing from there, Jesus went along by the Sea of Galilee, and having gone up to the mountain, He was sitting there.   And great multitudes came to Him, bringing with them {those who were} lame, crippled, blind, dumb, and many others, and they laid them down at His feet; and He healed them,   so that the multitude marveled as they saw the dumb speaking, the crippled restored, and the lame walking, and the blind seeing; and they glorified the God of Israel.

3John 11   Beloved, do not imitate what is evil, but what is good.   The one who does good is of God; the one who does evil has not seen God.

NOTES:

EXT. CAMPFIRE. NIGHT: (SCENE 8)

JUDAS: You know people spend their whole
                    lives waiting for somebody to come into
                    their life that can do some good. So, it's
                    no secret to me who Jesse is. I mean,
                    once you get the people to follow you,
                    believe in you, then you got it.

ANDY: Got what?

JUDAS: Power ... real power ... political,
                    economic... and by this time next year
                    we can have the whole damn world in
                    our pocket ... and own it ... too.

                    (JESSE and DISCIPLES walk up.)

JESSE: And then what?

                    (JUDAS walks away.)

JAMES: What's going on?

ANDY: Seems like all he ever talks about is
                    power.

JESSE: Well, there's nothing wrong with power
                    in itself ... it's how you use it.

                    (JUDAS walks away from camp.
                    VOICES of DISCIPLES heard in
                    background. JUDAS walks down hill
                    toward river)

JESSE: (VO) Hey you got any food left?

EXT. CAMPFIRE. NIGHT (CONT'D):

ANDY:

(VO) Caught a bunch of trout. You should see what we caught today, I mean ... you want some? Etc.

JUDAS:

I know he's here for a reason ... I know that. The things I can do with that kind of a power. One day, somebody's gonna offer him the world. I'm gonna make sure he takes it. I'm gonna make sure ... he takes it!

STUDY SCENE:
NO. 8

In this scene its obvious Judas thinks he knows who Jesse is, and has become totally obsessed with the possibility of using Jesse's ever increasing popularity as a means to climb to the top for his own personal gain; both, political and economic.

The one thing Judas does know, is that Jesse's here for a reason. Exactly what, he doesn't know; however, he does sense an incredible power and totally believes that Jesse will soon rise to a position where he could possibly be a world leader.... if not, the world leader.

Obviously Judas' vision of Jesse was skewed by his own ambition... unlike Simeon ... a man who spent his whole life doing good and looking for the consolation of Israel.

> *Luke 2:25   And behold, there was a man in Jerusalem whose name was Simeon; and this man was righteous and devout, looking for the consolation of Israel; and the Holy Spirit was upon him. And it had been revealed to him by the Holy Spirit that he would not see death before he had seen the Lord's Christ.   And he came in the Spirit into the temple; and when the parents brought in the child Jesus, to carry out for Him the custom of the Law, then he took Him into his arms, and blessed God, and said, "Now Lord, Thou dost let Thy bond-servant depart In peace, according to Thy word; For my eyes have seen Thy salvation, Which Thou hast prepared in the presence of all peoples,   A LIGHT OF REVELATION TO THE GENTILES, And the glory of Thy people Israel."*

1. How would you view a young man, 30 yrs. old, performing miracle after miracle... while at the same time ... your dreams of freedom, even religious freedom, are being suppressed?

2. How healthy is our spiritual climate today?

3. Would you be able to recognize Jesus, within your own environment, if He appeared among us for the first time? Was Jesus recognized and/or followed by everyone He encountered... even those in his own home town ... or household?

> *Matt. 13:54-58 He came to His hometown and began to teach the people in their synagogue, so that they were astounded and said, "Where did this man get this wisdom and these deeds of power? Is not this the carpenter's son? Is not his mother called Mary? And are not his brothers James and Joseph and Simon and Judas? And are not all his sisters with us? Where then did this man get all this?" And they took offense at him. But Jesus said to them,* **"Prophets are not without honor, except in their hometown, and among their own kin, and in their own house."** *And He did not do many deeds of power there, because of their unbelief.*

> *John 7:3-5 His brothers therefore said to Him, "Depart from here, and go into Judea, that Your disciples also may behold Your works which You are doing. "For no one does anything in secret, when he himself seeks to be {known} publicly. If You do these things, show Yourself to the world." For not even His brothers were believing in Him.*

4. Knowing about Jesus is NOT the same as "knowing Him".

> *John 10:27 **"My sheep hear my voice. I know them, and <u>they follow me</u>."***

5. In order to follow Him, you need to know His voice personally. Hearsay is not enough .. just as you can not experience birth second hand.

> *John 10:4-5 **"When he puts forth all his own, he goes before them, and the sheep follow him because they know his voice. And the strangers they simply will not follow, but will flee from him because they do not know the voice of strangers."***

Jesus was not opposed to money or power, rather, to the way that they were used by people (to control one another). He used all of His power, on this earth, to bring glory to His Father and our Father, and to show us the way to Him. That power was ... and is ... His Love.

NOTES:

EXT. CAMPGROUND. DAY: (SCENE 9 & 10)

	(JESSE contemplates. JUDAS and ANDY fishing in the stream. JAMES, JOHN and PETER gather in wood. JESSE approaches.)
JOHN:	JESSE!
JESSE:	Hey, got enough wood?
	(DISCIPLES laughs.)
JESSE:	Why don't you take a walk with me?
JOHN:	Where are we going?
JESSE:	Oh, to the top of the mountain.
JAMES:	(Laughs) Why?
JESSE:	Because it's time for you to see who I am ... and why I've come.
JOHN:	I know who you are.
JESSE:	(OS) Who am I, John?
JOHN:	(funny smile) You're a great teacher ... and a healer.
JESSE:	Well, some see me as the Messiah. Others see me as just a teacher. Come, follow me.
	(OS) Come on. (IN FRAME) Come on.
	(They follow him up the mountain.)

EXT. PATH UP THE MOUNTAIN. DAY:

JOHN: Jesse, how much further?

JESSE: 'Till we reach the top.

JOHN: Wonderful.

JESSE: When you climb a mountain, keep your eye on the summit .. not on how far it is.

EXT. MOUNTAIN TOP. DAY:

JESSE: Stand back. (JESSE walks up on top of a huge boulder) Don't be afraid of what you're about to see.

                        (JOHN sees cloud formation.) , (Wind begins to pick up)

JOHN: Peter, look.

                        (Sky grows dark and ominous. Lightening flashes all around DISCIPLES. JESSE stretches out his arms towards the sky and begins to glow with intense white light.)

GOD: (VO) This is my Son, with whom I'm well pleased. Listen to him!

                        (Lightning flashes and TWO SPIRITS descend from the clouds and materialize on either side of JESSE. JESSE talks with them and the TWO SPIRITS ascend back up into the clouds.... JESSE returns to normal and smiles)

JESSE: It's OK. There's nothing to be afraid of!

EXT. MOUNTAIN TOP. DAY (CONT'D):

	(JOHN faints and falls backward to the ground.)
JESSE:	(Lifts John's head) John, my friend.
JOHN:	Are we all dead?
	(ALL laugh.)
JESSE:	No John, we're not dead.
JOHN:	Oh, good.
JESSE:	Would you like to sit up?
JOHN:	Yeah!
	(JESSE looks at the disciples)
JESSE:	Who am I?
PETER:	You're Christ, the Son of God.
JESSE:	Then you've been blessed ... because flesh and blood did not reveal this to you, but my Father in heaven. And I say to you that you are a stone ... and upon this rock, I will build my church ... and the gates of hell shall not prevail against it. I will give you the keys to the kingdom ... and whatever you bind on earth will be bound in heaven ... and whatever you loose on earth will be loosed in heaven. In a little while, my life will be sacrificed ... for the sins of mankind. And I will descend into hell,

EXT. MOUNTAIN TOP. DAY (CONT'D):

JESSE (CONT'D):	defeat death ... and free the captives. On the third day, I .. will .. rise!
PETER:	NO! You don't have to die. You're the Son of God!
JESSE:	(Pointing to PETER) Satan!
PETER:	Who could kill you?
	(JESSE puts his finger on PETER'S CHEST and AS PETER STUMBLES backward)
JESSE:	SATAN! Get behind me! You're a stumbling block to me! It isn't God's interests you have in mind... it's man's. My Father created this world for me ... so that no one would have to live in darkness. So think of me as light ... and Satan as darkness. Where there is light, darkness can't exist. Every light needs a light switch ... and I will make you mine ... and you will tell the world about me. Anything you see me do, you can do in my name ... and if you have enough faith in me, you can do even greater things. Always remember, do not fear those who are able to kill the body and not the soul ... rather fear Him who can kill both body ... and soul ... in hell.
	(JESSE walks away ... then turns to the DISCIPLES)

EXT. MOUNTAIN TOP. DAY (CONT'D):

JESSE (CONT'D):   Tell no one what you saw here today, until I have risen from the dead.

STUDY SCENE:
NO. 9 & 10

As this scene begins, we observe Jesse, deep in thought, sitting alone by the stream.

> *Luke 5:15-16   But the news about Him was spreading even farther, and great multitudes were gathering to hear {Him} and to be healed of their sicknesses. But He Himself would {often} slip away to the wilderness and pray.*

> *Luke 9:18-19   And it came about that while He was praying alone, the disciples were with Him, and He questioned them, saying, **"Who do the multitudes say that I am?"** And they answered and said, "John the Baptist, and others {say} Elijah; but others, that one of the prophets of old has risen again."*

1. The disciples knew who the multitudes thought that Jesus was. That is why Jesse said to Peter, James and John; "It's time for you to see who I am, and why I've come?

> *Matt. 17:1   Jesus took with Him Peter and James and John his brother, and brought them up to a high mountain by themselves.*

2. As the disciples climbed, they became tired and grumpy as to how much further they had to go. What did Jesse mean when he said: "When you climb a mountain, keep your eyes on the summit, not on how far it is."

> *1Cor. 10:13   No testing has overtaken you that is not common to everyone. God is faithful, and He will not let you be tested beyond your strength, but with the testing He will also provide the way out so that you may be able to endure it.*

Hebr. 12:1   ...   and let us run with perseverance the race that is set before us,

Phil. 3:13-14 ... reaching forward to what lies ahead, I press on toward the goal for the prize of the upward call of God in Christ Jesus.

Phil. 4:13   I can do all things through Him who strengthens me.

3. Once they reached the summit, they were surrounded by the grandeur of the view. Jesse walks up on the top of a huge boulder and cautions them saying: "Stand back ... don't be afraid of what you are about to see."

Luke 9:34   And while he was saying this, a cloud formed and {began} to overshadow them; and they were afraid as they entered the cloud.

4. Both the spiritual and natural eyes of the disciples needed to be opened as to who Jesse was and why he had come.

Matt. 17:2-3   And He was transfigured before them; and His face shone like the sun, and His garments became as white as light. And behold, Moses and Elijah appeared to them, talking with Him.

*Matt. 17:5-8   While he was still speaking, be-hold, a bright cloud overshadowed them; and behold, a voice out of the cloud, saying, **'This is My Beloved Son, with whom I am well pleased; Listen to Him!'.** And when the disciples heard this, they fell on their faces and were much afraid. And Jesus came to them and touched them and said, **'Arise, and do not be afraid'.** And lifting up their*

*eyes, they saw no one, except Jesus Himself
alone.*

Jesse had given the disciples an enormous foundation for
their faith walk. Along with the teachings, they received another
confirmation as to who Jesse is by his Father who spoke to them
from the cloud. The sight of the cloud and perhaps the sound of
God's voice was obviously too much for John ... as he fainted.
When he came to, he wasn't quite sure if they were all dead or not.

Throughout the bible when God audibly spoke to His
people, they were always frightened by it. God has never stopped
talking to us. One of the greatest ways He talks to us today is
through His Word.... the Bible.

> *Rom. 10:17   So faith {comes} from hearing, and
> hearing by the word of God (Christ).*

5. Jesse often asked the disciples questions because their hearing
the answers was necessary to their growth. So again, he asks them:
"Who am I?"

> *Matt. 16:15-19   He said to them, **'But who do
> you say that I am?'** Simon Peter answered, 'You
> are the Messiah, the Son of the living God.' And
> Jesus answered him, **'Blessed are you, Simon son
> of Jonah! For flesh and blood has not revealed
> this to you, but my Father in heaven. And I tell
> you, you are Peter, and on this rock I will build
> My church, and the gates of Hades will not
> prevail against it. I will give you the keys of the
> kingdom of heaven, and whatever you bind on
> earth will be bound in heaven, and whatever you
> loose on earth will be loosed in heaven'."**

> *Matt. 16:21-23   From that time on Jesus began
> to show His disciples that He must go to
> Jerusalem and undergo great suffering at the*

hands of the elders and chief priests and scribes, and be killed, and on the third day be raised.

6. Peter rebukes Jesse urging him to escape the cross.

> *Matt. 16:22   And Peter took Him aside and began to rebuke Him, saying, "God forbid it, Lord! This must never happen to You."*

7. Jesse's response to Peter showed that he was totally committed to God's will and could not be swayed.

> *Matt. 16:23   But He turned and said to Peter,* **"Get behind me, Satan! You are a stumbling block to me; for you are not setting your mind on God's interests, but mans."**

8. When Jesse was speaking with the group, he made the follow-ing statements in order to equip them with knowledge, wisdom and power ... for what they will encounter.

   A. "My father created this world for me so that no one would have to live in darkness."

   > *John 1:1-4   In the beginning was the Word, and the Word was with God, and the Word was God. He was in the beginning with God. All things came into being through Him, and without Him not one thing came into being. What has come into being in Him was life, and the life was the light of all people.*

   B. "So think of me as light. and Satan as darkness. Where there is light, darkness can't exist."

> *John 8:12   Again Jesus spoke to them, saying, "***I am the light of the world. Whoever follows Me will never walk in darkness but shall have the light of life.***"*

C. "Every light needs a light switch, and I will make you mine; And, you will tell the world about me."

> *Mark 16:15   And He said to them, **"Go into all the world and proclaim the good news to the whole creation."***

D. "Anything you see me do, you can do in my name. And, if you have enough faith in me, you can do even greater things."

> *John 14:12   **"Very truly, I tell you, the one who believes in Me will also do the works that I do and, in fact, ... will do greater works than these, because I am going to the Father."***

E. "Do not fear those who are able to kill the body, but not the soul ... rather, fear Him who can kill both body and soul in hell."

> *Matt. 10:28   **"Do not fear those who kill the body but cannot kill the soul; rather fear Him who can destroy both soul and body in hell."***

F. "Tell no one what you saw here today, until I have risen from the dead."

> *Mark 9:9   As they were coming down the mountain, He ordered them to tell no one about what they had seen, until after the Son of Man had risen from the dead.*

NOTES:

EXT. BEACH. DAY: (SCENE 11 & 12)

JESSE: (OS) You have heard that you should
                          love your neighbor and hate your enemy
                          ... but what reward is in that?

                          (IN FRAME) I am telling you to love
                          your enemies ... and pray and forgive
                          those who persecute you.

                          (OS) Do you expect God to do for you
                          what you are not willing to do for
                          others? Since God is your Father,
                          shouldn't you be a reflection of Him?

                          (IN FRAME) Anything that lasts is
                          built on a solid foundation. My words
                          give life ...

                          (OS) and anything built upon My words
                          will last forever ... but if you reject Me,

                          (IN FRAME) you're building on sand.
                          When the winds and floods come,
                          whatever you built on

                          (OS) will be undermined and fall to
                          ruin.

PETER: Jesse, they're hungry and cold.

JESSE: Bring Me the bread and cheese from the
                          back of Judas' van.

JOHN: (Laughing) I think Peter's the wrong
                          one to send for the food.

JUDAS: Jesse, there's only a couple of loaves of

EXT. BEACH. DAY (CONT'D):

JUDAS (CONT'D):	bread and some cheese. It's not even enough to feed Peter, much less ... all these people.

(JESSE pats child on head then goes to JOHN. Peter and Andy go to the van for food. Background sounds of crowd murmuring. JESSE walks back to JUDAS.) |
| JESSE: | Well, take it. Go on, take it! |
| JUDAS: | Not me. |
| JESSE: | (Places his hand on JUDAS' SHOULDER)

Only when you're willing to give, what little you have ... will God use it, multiply it and teach you the true meaning ...of prosperity.

(SONG **"HE'S JUST A MAN WITH A BAND AND A MAGIC SHOW"** PLAYS OVER REST OF SCENE).

JUDAS passes out loaves and cheese, to the crowd, which multiply miraculously! As they do so, DeCARMO is seen in the distance photographing them. |
| SONG LYRICS: | (VO) YESTERDAY I MET A MAN I EVEN JOINED THE BAND ... OF THE TRAVELING MAN AND, PEOPLE COME FROM MILES AROUND TO SEE THE SHOW ... |

EXT. BEACH. DAY (CONT'D):

SONG LYRICS: WOULDN'T YOU KNOW

I HEARD THE PEOPLE SHOUT
THAT HE'S THE KING
BUT HE SHAKES HIS HEAD AND
SAYS HE JUST WANTS TO SHARE
A DREAM.

HE'S JUST A MAN WITH A BAND
AND A MAGIC SHOW
A MAN WITH A DREAM EVERY
BODY WANTS TO KNOW
BUT I'M THE ONLY ONE ... WHO
THINKS IT'S JUST A SHOW
BUT THERE'S SOMETHING DEEP
INSIDE THAT SAYS I WANNA
KNOW

WE TOOK THE SHOW FROM TOWN
TO TOWN
I WATCHED HIM HEAL THE BLIND
CHANGE WATER TO WINE
AND, YOU DON'T KNOW WHAT
WENT THROUGH MY HEAD
WITH JUST THE SOUND OF HIS
VOICE
I SAW HIM RAISE THE DEAD

I HEARD THE PEOPLE SHOUT ..
HE'S THE KING
BUT HE SHAKES HIS HEAD AND
SAYS HE JUST WANTS TO SHARE
A DREAM

HE'S JUST A MAN WITH A BAND
AND A MAGIC SHOW

EXT. BEACH. DAY (CONT'D):

SONG LYRIC (CONT'D):

> A MAN WITH A DREAM
> EVERYBODY WANTS TO KNOW
> AND I'M THE ONLY ONE WHO
> THINKS IT'S JUST A SHOW
> BUT THERE'S SOMETHING DEEP
> INSIDE THAT SAYS I GOTTA KNOW
>
> AND IT WAS THEN HE CAME TO
> ME
> AND WITH HIS EYES ... OH, HE
> LOOKED RIGHT THROUGH ME
> AND THEN HE SHARED HIS
> DREAM WITH ME
> HE SAID IF YOU BELIEVE ... AH,
> YOU'LL NEVER BE LONELY
>
> I HEARD THE PEOPLE SHOUT
> THAT HE'S THE KING
> BUT HE SHAKES HIS HEAD AND
> SAYS
> HE JUST WANTS TO SHARE
> A DREAM
>
> HE'S JUST A MAN WITH A BAND
> AND A MAGIC SHOW
> A MAN WITH A DREAM
> EVERYBODY WANTS TO KNOW

STUDY SCENE:
NO. 11 & 12

Whenever possible, Jesus took the opportunity to teach and prepare a proper foundation for life not only for his followers, but for everyone who was willing to listen. If they received His teachings, in their every day life, they would be much richer for it, for it is truly "more blessed to give than to receive".

1. In this scene Jesse is dealing with the following scriptures that are difficult for most people to put into action:

> *Matt. 5:43-46* **"You have heard that it was said, 'You shall love your neighbor and hate your enemy.' But I say to you, Love your enemies and pray for those who persecute you, so that you may be children of your Father in heaven; for He makes his sun rise on the evil and on the good, and sends rain on the righteous and on the unrighteous. For if you love those who love you, what reward do you have? Do not even the tax collectors do the same?"**

> *Prov. 27:19* *As in water face reflects face, <u>so the heart of man reflects man.</u>*

> *Luke 6:46-49* **"Why do you call Me 'Lord, Lord,' and do not do what I tell you? I will show you what someone is like who comes to Me, hears My words, and acts on them. That one is like a man building a house, who dug deeply and laid the foundation on rock; when a flood arose, the river burst against that house but could not shake it, because it had been well built. But the one who hears and does not act is like a man who built a house on the ground without a foundation. When the river burst against it, immediately it fell, and great was the ruin of that house."**

> *John 6:63 **"It is the spirit that gives life; the flesh
> is useless. The words that I have spoken to you are
> spirit and life."***

2. Could the feeding of the multitude be one of the first miracles
involving the disciples? How does the following scripture expose
the humanity of the disciples?

> *Matt. 15:32-37   Then Jesus called His disciples to
> Him and said, **"I have compassion for the crowd,
> because they have been with Me now for three
> days and have nothing to eat; and I do not want to
> send them away hungry, for they might faint on
> the way."**   The disciples said to Him, "Where are
> we to get enough bread in the desert to feed so great
> a crowd?" Jesus asked them, **"How many loaves
> <u>do you have?"</u>** They said, "Seven, and a few small
> fish." Then ordering the crowd to sit down on the
> ground, He took the seven loaves and the fish; and
> after giving thanks He broke them and gave them to
> the disciples, and the disciples gave them to the
> crowds. And all of them ate and were filled; and
> they took up the broken pieces left over, seven bas-
> kets full.*

Also:

> *Mark 6:34-44   As He went ashore, He saw a great
> crowd; and He had compassion for them, because
> they were like sheep without a shepherd; and He
> began to teach them many things. When it grew
> late, His disciples came to Him and said, "This is
> a deserted place, and the hour is now very late;
> send them away so that they may go into the sur-
> rounding country and villages and buy something
> for themselves to eat." But He answered them,
> **"You give them something to eat."** They said to*

Him, "Are we to go and buy two hundred denarii
worth of bread, and give it to them to eat?"
And He said to them, **"How many loaves do you
have? Go and see."** When they had found out,
they said, "Five, and two fish." Then He ordered
them to get all the people to sit down in groups on
the green grass. So they sat down in groups of
hundreds and of fifties. Taking the five loaves and
the two fish, He looked up to heaven, and blessed
and broke the loaves, and gave them to His disciples to set before the people; and He divided the
two fish among them all. And all ate and were
filled; and they took up twelve baskets full of
broken pieces and of the fish. Those who had
eaten the loaves numbered five thousand men.

3. When Jesse put his hand on Judas' shoulder, what do you sup-
pose he meant by; "Only when you're willing to give what little
you have, will God use it, multiply it and teach you the true meaning of prosperity?"

1Kgs. 17:10-16 So he set out and went to Zarephath.
When he came to the gate of the town, a widow was
there gathering sticks; he called to her and said,
"Bring me a little water in a vessel, so that I may
drink." As she was going to bring it, he called to
her and said, "Bring me a morsel of bread in your
hand." But she said, "As the LORD your God lives,
I have nothing baked, only a handful of meal in a
jar, and a little oil in a jug; I am now gathering a
couple of sticks, so that I may go home and prepare
it for myself and my son, that we may eat it, and
die." Elijah said to her, "Do not be afraid; go and
do as you have said; but first make me a little cake
of it and bring it to me, and afterwards make some
thing for yourself and your son. For thus says the
LORD the God of Israel: "The jar of meal will not

be emptied and the jug of oil will not fail until the day that the LORD sends rain on the earth." She went and did as Elijah said, so that she as well as he and her household ate for many days. The jar of meal was not emptied, neither did the jug of oil fail, according to the word of the LORD that he spoke by Elijah.

A little boy gives all that he has.

*John 6:9-11   "There is a boy here who has five barley loaves and two fish. But what are they among so many people?" Jesus said, **"Make the people sit down."** Now there was a great deal of grass in the place; so they sat down, about five thousand in all.   Then Jesus took the loaves, and when He had given thanks, He distributed them to those who were seated; so also the fish, as much as they wanted.*

*Luke 6:38   **"Give, and it will be given to you. A good measure, pressed down, shaken together, running over, will be put into your lap; for the measure you give will be the measure you get back."***

4. During the feeding of the multitude and as the song plays over it, we also notice DeCarmo as if "hiding", yet all the while taking pictures of everyone on the beach. Why was he there?

> *Phil. 3:21   For they all seek after their own interest, not those of Christ Jesus.*

5. The disciples were given authority by Jesus to go out, preach the gospel, take authority over unclean spirits and every kind of sickness. Judas was given the same authority.

Mark 6:7   He called the twelve and began to send them out two by two, and gave them authority over the unclean spirits.

Matt. 10:1   Then Jesus summoned His twelve disciples and gave them authority over unclean spirits, to cast them out, and to cure every disease and every sickness.

Mark 3:13-19   He went up the mountain and called to Him those whom He wanted, and they came to Him. And He appointed twelve, whom He also named apostles, to be with Him, and to be sent out to proclaim the message, and to have authority to cast out demons. So He appointed the twelve: Simon (to whom he gave the name Peter); James son of Zebedee and John the brother of James (to whom he gave the name Boanerges, that is, Sons of Thunder);   and Andrew, and Philip, and Bartholomew, and Matthew, and Thomas, and James son of Alphaeus, and Thaddaeus, and Simon the Cananaean, and Judas Iscariot, who betrayed Him. Then He went home;

The song, **"He's Just A Man With A Band And A Magic Show"** describes Judas' inner struggle with himself. Until now he's only seen miracles taking place; however, now he has become a participant, performing them as well. He has seen followers flocking to Jesus, wanting to make Him a king. Jesus already has a kingdom and is teaching His followers how they can become better citizens. To some, Jesus may have appeared as performing magic (Matt. 12:22-24), but they were not "believers". Did Judas believe (John 6:64), though he was seeing things take place before his eyes ... knowing also that Jesus sees right through him and his loneliness?

NOTES

EXT. INNER CITY STREETS. NIGHT: (SCENE 13)

	(A limo drives up. ASA gets out and makes her way through crowd of street type people to JESSE.)
ASA:	Excuse me, Jesse? I'm Asa, may I speak with you? I'm representing my employer, Mr. Arthur Cunningham ... he's quite impressed with you. He's flying in from the West Coast and will be at his home tomorrow evening for a special and private gathering. The meeting is in regard to you. Mr. Cunningham would like you to be his guest tomorrow evening.
JESSE:	That would be fine.
ASA:	Wonderful, then I will pick you up.
JESSE:	As you wish.
	(ASA leaves. JESSE walks and stops at the corner of an ALLEY. As several PROSTITUTES come around the corner, JESSE reaches out and takes one of the young PROSTITUTES by the arm ... turns her around ......looks deep in her eyes).
JESSE:	(Whispers) This is no life for you. Find Christ in your heart, you'll be my family I love you.

EXT. INNER CITY STREETS. NIGHT (CONT'D):

> (The young PROSTITUTE turns and is
> obviously deeply moved... JESSE walks
> on ... stops ... looks up ALLEY ... shakes
> his head in sadness and lets out a SIGH.
> JESSE walks up the ALLEY and sits
> down beside a passed out wino ...
> possibly a homeless person. He looks at
> him ... looks up ..., sighs and just sits
> contemplating under the alley light.)

**EXT. STREET OUTSIDE OF CUNNINGHAM'S HOME.
DAY:**

> (A parade of limos drive up to building.
> Dignitaries from around the world enter
> building. NO DIALOGUE.)

STUDY SCENE:
NO. 13

1. The importance of the scene with the young prostitute is to establish the fact that Jesus loves us. Too many people, especially the youth, feel they aren't good enough for Jesus to love them. They don't know to ask for His forgiveness unless someone explains to them the love of God, and how He wants to not only forgive their sins, but simply love them just as they are. Although God hates the sin in our life, there is no sin (other than blasphemy against the Holy Spirit) that He won't forgive.

> *Matt. 12:31* **"Therefore I tell you, people will be forgiven for every sin and blasphemy, <u>but blaspheny against the Holy Spirit will not be forgiven.</u>"**

Jesse offers the prostitute a choice. She can continue to look at herself in her present state, or choose to see herself as he sees her, with Christ in her heart, as part of His family.

> *Matt. 12:50* **"For whoever does the will of My Father who is in heaven, he is My brother and sister and mother."**

Is she really any different than the rest of us in that;

A. We are all created in the image of God.

> *Gen. 1:27*   *And God created man in His own image, in the image of God, He created him; male and female He created them.*

B. We are <u>all</u> sinners.

> *Rom. 3:23* <u>*For all have sinned and fall short of the glory of God.*</u>

> *John 8:7 ... **"Let anyone among you who is without sin be the first to throw a stone at her."***
>
> *John 8:11 ..And Jesus said, **"Neither do I condemn you. Go your way. From now on sin no more."***

    C. The wages of sin is death. God can forgive us and reinstate us, in His favor, through the cross of Christ... and in no other way. Forgiveness which is so easy for us to accept cost the agony of Calvary. <u>We should never forget at what cost to God His forgiveness was made available to us</u>.

> *Rom. 6:23 For the wages of sin is death, but the free gift of God is eternal life in Christ Jesus our Lord.*
>
> *John 3:16 **"For God so loved the world that He gave His only Son, so that everyone who believes in Him may not perish but may have eternal life."***

    D. How do we receive eternal life?

> *Rom. 10:9-10 That if you <u>confess with your mouth</u> Jesus as Lord, and <u>believe in your heart</u> that God raised Him from the dead, <u>you shall be saved</u>; for with the heart man believes, resulting in righteousness, and with the mouth he confesses, resulting in salvation.*

2. The significance of Jesse sitting down beside the person in the alley, is to let us know that he is always with us and that there is no burden of ours too heavy for him to carry.

> *Matt. 11:28 **"Come to me, all you that are weary and are carrying heavy burdens, and I will give you rest."***

Matt. 6:25-26 **"For this reason I say to you, do not be anxious for your life, as to what you shall eat, or what you shall drink; nor for your body, as to what you shall put on. Is not life more than food, and the body than clothing? Look at the birds of the air, that they do not sow, neither do they reap, nor gather into barns, and yet your heavenly Father feeds them. Are you not worth much more than they?"**

3. Through Jesus Christ we not only receive eternal life, resulting in salvation, but also receive a promise that if we believe we will never be alone.

Hebr. 13:5 ... for He has said, **"I will never leave you or forsake you."**

Matt. 28:20 .... **"And remember, I am with you always, to the end of the age."**

NOTES:

INT. CUNNINGHAM'S HOME. DAY: (SCENE #14 & 15)

(Secret Service men open doors of meeting room to JESSE.)

CUNNINGHAM: How very kind of you to come. Arthur Cunningham ...

JESSE: Jesse.

CUNNINGHAM: Jesse! (Shakes Jesse's hand) I'm sure you recognize several of our more renowned world leaders ... all in one room to pay homage to one man ... you. Why don't you sit next to Asa. Make yourself comfortable.

(Looks at DISCIPLES who continue to stand)

Gentlemen, please, find a seat.

(JESSE motions to the DISCIPLES to be seated.. as DISCIPLES are being seated, CUNNINGHAM walks over to a large world map)

This world of ours is a simple place to run, actually. We, ah, control the East and we control the West ... you add in a few wars and, uh, everything falls into balance. At present, however, it seems that the world is hopelessly out of balance. The Communists can't seem to control their own party anymore. They're suffering from economic and consumer failure and the people don't know who or what to believe in

INT. CUNNINGHAM'S HOME. DAY (CONT'D):

CUNNINGHAM (CONT'D):   anymore. The West continues to hold its own, and flex its muscle. All the other countries have a lot of leaders with different ideas and very confused followers. However, there is one common denominator in every single country. The people want a leader ... a strong, magical, life saving king,

(OS) if you will.

JESSE: (Looking at world leaders, Ponerous and Cunningham) Is this how you see me?

(OS) Is this the reason for the invitation?

CUNNINGHAM: Why, yes, as a matter of fact, it is. I, above all men, easily recognize authority and power in another. I can't say that I prize that authority from which your power comes ... but I would have to be totally blind not to recognize the fact that you have struck a chord in the hearts of people

(OS) throughout the world. The desire is already there in the people to follow you. You already have the people ... the power, Jesse.

(IN FRAME) We have the Universal Organization and the ability to harness that power ... for the good of not just one, but all mankind.

INT. CUNNINGHAM'S HOME. DAY (CONT'D):

JESSE: The world I came to serve ... is not the world you serve. You don't see me as I am ... you see me only according to ... your needs.

PONEROUS: (OS) Our need

(IN FRAME) my young friend, is for you to stop this fanaticism ... and learn how to be a team player.

JESSE: (Jumping up angry) **I'VE COME TO HELP**! ...

(Looking into the eyes of PONEROUS) To bring light into a world that **YOU**

(pointing to PONEROUS)

are **destroying** and **deceiving** with your brand of **religiosity**! The weak, need strength, the strong need tenderness ... the tempted and fallen need salvation ... the righteous need pity for sinners, the fighters need a leader and the lonely... the lonely simply need a friend.

(OS) Only **God** can be all these things.

PONEROUS: (Scowling) Are you saying **you are God**?

CUNNINGHAM: Ponerous..

JESSE: (OS) Is that who you think I am?

INT. CUNNINGHAM'S HOME. DAY (CONT'D):

PONEROUS: I think you reek of back alleys of blasphemy! (OS) God doesn't associate with whores and procurers and spend time with scum.

(IN FRAME) I could promote you! ... turn you into something wonderful ... make you... beautiful!

JESSE: And what does rotting flesh know of beauty?

(OS) You're blind

(IN FRAME) to yourself, and to the destruction with which your followers are being led. Darkness can't exist where there's light ... and YOU - THRIVE in **darkness**! I am the light you seek to destroy.

(OS) My very presence exposes you and your followers for who you are. And **YOU**!

(IN FRAME pointing his finger at CUNNINGHAM) you seek to control the very thing that controls you.

(CUNNINGHAM grabs his wrist as if it hurts.... Jesse walks around to the head of the table and stands behind JUDAS).

The world has always had a leader ... trouble is no one wants to listen, much less follow. Let's get out of here.

INT. CUNNINGHAM'S HOME. DAY (CONT'D):

	(JESSE and all DISCIPLES but JUDAS exit. JUDAS stays behind)
CUNNINGHAM:	(Talking to PONEROUS and DeCARMO) You realize the people love him ... with or without our help.
PONEROUS:	It may be expedient that one man should die, that we might save a nation.
DeCARMO:	(Shaken) What?

STUDY SCENE:
NO. 14 & 15

In this scene, Cunningham has assembled several world leaders, as well as, Ponerous. Cunningham recognizes Jesse's power and popularity and regards him as a strong, magical, life saving king. He has high hopes of Jesse's joining their organization for the good of all mankind. The meeting was for a single purpose ... to offer Jesse the world.

1. Was Jesus ever offered the world?

> *Matt. 4:8 Again, the devil took Him to a very high mountain and showed Him all the kingdoms of the world and their splendor; and he said to Him, "All these I will give You, if You will fall down and worship me." Jesus said to him, **"Away with you, Satan! for it is written, Worship the Lord your God, and serve only Him.' "***

2. Did some of Jesus' followers recognize Him as a King?

> *Acts 17:7 They are all acting contrary to the decrees of the emperor, saying that there is another King named Jesus.*

A. In response to Cunningham's offer to join their organization, Jesse said; "The world I came to serve is not the world you serve."

> *John 18:36 Jesus answered, **"My kingdom is not of this world"**...*

B. Exposing their hearts and motives, Jesse continued; "You don't see me as I am, you see me only according to your needs."

> *John 6:14-15 When the people saw the sign that He had done, they began to say, "This is indeed the prophet who is to come into the world." When Jesus realized that they were about to come and <u>take Him by force to make Him King</u>, He withdrew again to the mountain by Himself.*

3. Unsuccessfully, Ponerous tries hard to convince Jesse and the world leaders as to what he wants saying; "Our need my young friend, is for you to stop this fanaticism and learn how to be a team player;" Jesse, knowing the deceptiveness of Ponerous, speaks his mind ... stating the facts:

A. "I've come to help! to bring **light** into a world that **you** are **destroying and deceiving** with **your brand of religiosity**."

> *Matt. 15:6-9 "So, <u>for the sake of your tradition</u>, you make void the word of God. You hypocrites! Isaiah prophesied rightly about you when he said: 'This people honors me with their lips, but their hearts are far from me; in vain do they worship me, teaching human precepts as doctrines.' "*

> *Matt. 23:13 "But woe to you, scribes and Pharisees, hypocrites! For you lock people out of the kingdom of heaven. For you do not go in yourselves, and when others are going in, you stop them."*

> *Matt. 23:23 "Woe to you, scribes and Pharisees, hypocrites! For you tithe mint, dill, and cummin, and have neglected the weightier matters of the law: justice and mercy and faith. It is these you ought to have practiced without neglecting the others."*

> *Matt. 23:25   **"Woe to you, scribes and Pharisees, hypocrites! For you clean the outside of the cup and of the plate, but inside they are full of greed and self-indulgence."***
>
> *Matt. 23:29-33   **"Woe to you, scribes and Pharisees, hypocrites! For you build the tombs of the prophets and decorate the graves of the righteous, and say, 'If we had been {living} in the days of our fathers, we would not have been partners with them in {shedding} the blood of the prophets.' "Consequently you bear witness against yourselves, that you are sons of those who murdered the prophets. "Fill up then the measure {of the guilt} of your fathers. "You serpents, you brood of vipers, how shall you escape the sentence of hell? "***
>
> *John 12:46   **"I have come as light into the world, so that every one who believes in Me should not remain in the darkness."**.*

4. Knowing the hearts of men and their tremendous need for strength, courage, friendship, leadership, etc., Jesse also states; "Only God can be all these things;" Poneous glares at Jesse and asks;

   A. "Are you saying you are God?"

   > *Matt. 26:63   Then the high priest said to Him, "I put you under oath before the living God, tell us if you are the Messiah, the Son of God."*

5. What was Jesse's response to Ponerous?

   A. "Is that who you think I am?"

>*Matt. 26:64 Jesus said to him,* **"You have said so. "**

6. Ponerous never recognizes the fact that he <u>IS</u> speaking to God in the flesh. All he can think of is his overinflated ego and lofty position ... and responds accordingly; "I think you reek of back alleys and blasphemy! God doesn't associate with whores and procurers and spend time with scum. I could promote you! ... turn you into something wonderful! ... make you beautiful!" Much like Ponerous, the Pharisees questioned the disciples.

>*Matt. 9:11 Why is your teacher eating with the tax-gatherers and sinners?*

7. Jesse responds to Ponerous? "What does rotting flesh know of beauty?"

>*Matt. 23:27* **"Woe to you, scribes and Pharisees, hypocrites! For you are like whitewashed tombs, which on the outside look beautiful, but inside they are full of the bones of the dead and of all kinds of filth."**

>*Matt. 15:14* **."they** *(the Pharisees)* **are blind guides of the blind. And if one blind person guides another, both will fall into a pit."**

>*John 8:12 Again Jesus spoke to them, saying,* **"I am the light of the world. Whoever follows Me will never walk in darkness but will have the light of life."**

>*John 3:19-20* **...."that the light has come into the world, and people loved darkness rather than light because their deeds were evil. For all who do evil hate the light and do not come to the light, so that their deeds may not be exposed."**

8. When Jesse looked at Cunningham, he saw a man already controlled by the insatiable power he was seeking; "And you, you seek to control the very thing that controls you."

> *Prov. 25:28 Like a city breached, without walls, is one who lacks control over his own spirit.*

9. Jesse was referring to God when he said; "The world has always had a leader, trouble is no one wants to listen, much less follow."

> *Ex. 20:1-5 Then God spoke all these words: "I am the LORD your God, who brought you out of the land of Egypt, out of the house of slavery; you shall have no other gods before Me. You shall not make for yourself an idol, whether in the form of anything that is in heaven above, or that is on the earth beneath, or that is in the water under the earth. You shall not bow down to them or worship them; for I the LORD your God am a jealous God, punishing children for the iniquity of parents, to the third and the fourth generation of those who reject Me."*

10. Why does Judas stay behind?

> *Matt. 26:16 And from that moment he began to look for an opportunity to betray Him.*

11. Why did Ponerous say; "It may be expedient that one man should die, that we might save a nation?"

> *John 11:49-53 But one of them, Caiaphas, who was high priest that year, said to them, "You know nothing at all! You do not understand that it is better for you to have one man die for the people than to have the whole nation destroyed. He did*

not say this on his own, but being high priest that year he prophesied that Jesus was about to die for the nation, and not for the nation only, but to gather into one the dispersed children of God. So from that day on they planned to put Him to death.

12. Why did DeCarmo say; "What"?

Matt. 21:46 But they feared the crowds, because they regarded Him as a prophet.

AS A SPECIAL NOTE OF INTEREST:

You may be interested to know that the scene where Cunningham walks around the table and talks about <u>the downfall of the Communist Party</u> was written under the influence of the Holy Spirit .... and <u>registered</u> at the writers guild in L.A. <u>in 1981</u>.... years before it ever happened.

NOTES:

EXT. DOCKS. DAY: (SCENE 16)

(JESSE and DISCIPLES return from a fishing trip. Unintelligible background conversation from them. DeCARMO and JACKSON watch from boathouse. JACKSON gets JESSE in sights of his high powered rifle, JESSE turns and looks at him. JACKSON is shaken and can't pull the trigger ... EJECTS the shell)

DeCARMO: What are you doing? Shoot him! Shoot him!

(JACKSON walks away up the stairs. DeCARMO comes after him).

(OS) How do I explain this?

(IN FRAME) Jackson! You heard what he said, he's going to kill us

(OS) both!!

JACKSON: Tell your (knocks DeCARMO down the stairs with rifle)

(OS) Tell your

(IN FRAME) pious, pompous friend to do it himself!

STUDY SCENE:
NO. 16

In this scene, Jesse and the disciples have just returned from a fishing trip. Other than Jesse, none of the disciples are aware that Jackson and DeCarmo are hiding beneath an old boathouse, waiting for the opportunity to kill Jesse.

1. Did anyone "really" ever try to kill Jesus before He was delivered to Pilot and Herod?

> *John 8:59   Therefore they picked up stones to throw at Him; but Jesus hid Himself, and went out of the temple.*
>
> *John 10:31   The Jews took up stones again to stone Him.*
>
> *John 10:39   Therefore they were seeking again to seize Him, and He eluded their grasp.*
>
> *Luke 4:28-30 And all in the synagogue were filled with rage as they heard these things;   and they rose up and cast Him out of the city, and led Him to the brow of the hill on which their city had been built, in order to throw Him down the cliff. But passing through their midst, He went His way.*

2. Was Jesse concerned when he found himself in Jackson's scope?

> *John 7:8   ..**"for My time has not yet fully come."***

3. When Jesse stopped, turned and looked straight into Jackson's scope, why couldn't Jackson pull the trigger and kill Jesse? Was he beginning to "see" things differently?

John 7:30 .... His hour had not yet come.

Eph. 5:6-7   Let no one deceive you with empty words, for because of these things the wrath of God comes on those who are disobedient. Therefore do not be associated with them.

Eph. 5:10   Try to find out what is pleasing to the Lord.

4, Why did Jackson say to DeCarmo; "Tell your pious pompus friend to do it himself?" Was it possible that he recognized the truth?

Eph. 5:11-14   Take no part in the unfruitful works of darkness, but instead expose them. For it is shameful even to mention what such people do secretly; but everything exposed by the light becomes visible, for everything that becomes visible is light. Therefore it says, Sleeper, awake! Rise from the dead, and Christ will shine on you."

5. Why was DeCarmo part of the assassination attempt?

John 11:47-48   So the chief priests and the Pharisees called a meeting of the council, and said, "What are we to do? This man is performing many signs. If we let Him go on like this, everyone will believe in Him, and the Romans will come and destroy both our holy place and our nation."

NOTES:

EXT. CARNIVAL. NIGHT: (SCENE 17)

BUTTONS THE CLOWN:

Oh, goody, here comes some more!

(SEVERAL CARNIVAL SCENES)

(ASA approaches JUDAS as he plays an arcade game.

JUDAS:

.. plays please ... (looks at Asa) I don't believe this. What the hell are you doing here?

ASA:

There has been a slight change in plans nothing to be concerned about. The silver bars are in your Atlanta office, just as you requested.

JUDAS:

So why didn't you give me a call and tell me this on the phone like you were supposed to?

ASA:

Jackson is causing us a problem, so we had to change our plans. If you see him, get in touch with me immediately. I will be at this number all night ... so, when you get the information we need, you know where I'll be ... and I don't care what time it is ... understand?

JUDAS:

Yea, I think so. I think so.

ASA:

Good.

STUDY SCENE::
NO. 17

This scene establishes the fact that Judas and Asa have made definite plans for something; However, Asa's plans seem to be changing because of Jackson's sudden change of heart, and she needs help in locating him.

1. What is the importance of Asa saying to Judas; "The silver bars are in your Atlanta office, just as you requested?" Why were they delivered to Judas?

> *John 11:57   Now the chief priests and the Pharisees had given orders that anyone who knew where Jesus was should let them know, so that they might arrest Him.*

> *John 13:2   The devil had already put it into the heart of Judas son of Simon Iscariot to betray Him.*

> *Matt. 26:14-16   Then one of the twelve, who was called Judas Iscariot, went to the chief priests and said, "<u>What will you give me if I betray Him to you</u>?" They paid him thirty pieces of silver. And from that moment he began to look for an opportunity to betray Him.*

2. What is the significance of "thirty pieces of silver?"

> *Matt. 27:9   Then was fulfilled what had been spoken through the prophet Jeremiah, "And they took the <u>thirty pieces of silver,</u> the price of the One on Whom a price had been set, on Whom some of the people of Israel had set a price."*

NOTES:

EXT. BEACH. NIGHT   (SCENE 18)

	(JESSE, JOHN, PETER and ANDY sit around campfire.)
PETER:	(OS) Something's wrong.
JESSE:	For many with whom I've come into contact, my cause is lost. Even those of you who I've gathered around me as a nucleus to carry on the truths that I've taught you, half believe and half doubt. In spite of all that I've taught you, Tonight you'll all forsake me. because you'll think I've failed,
	(OS) because I choose not to use material force to overcome my enemies.
PETER:	Jesse, I'll never forsake you. I know who you are. And nobody's gonna get to you unless they come through me first, NOBODY!
JESSE:	I know your heart is in the right place, but before you can be the rock that I've called you to be, you must overcome your greatest weakness, Peter,
	(OS) and that's fear.
	(IN FRAME) Tonight, Satan will sift you and before the night is over, you'll deny knowing me three times. The rest is up to the depth of your belief in the faith that you have in me. After tonight you must learn to walk by faith alone.

EXT. BEACH. NIGHT (CONT'D):

JESSE (CONT'D):   A final test must come to all who walk by faith. You must rely on me alone. Trust in no other and seek no other help.

(OS) Expect storms if you're to do my work. Because of your love, friendship and bond to do my work, you'll excite the enemy the malice and hatred of all those who are not on my side.

(IN FRAME) The enemy attacks the fortress ... the stronghold, never the desert waste. The group looks to you ...

(OS) so trust in the Spirit that I will send you ... not what you see, or what your present circumstances dictate.

(IN FRAME) If you truly love me, you'll survive ... and you'll carry my message.

(Reprise of first scene - helicopters landing, armed men surrounding JESSE and DISCIPLES.)

ARMED MEN: Stop right there!! Freeze! Stop or you're dead!! Freeze, don't move. Stay where you are!!!

(ARMED MEN encircle JESSE. JUDAS walks up to him.)

JUDAS: (Contemplates... then SCREAMS) WHY??!!

EXT. BEACH. NIGHT (CONT'D):

    (JUDAS hugs JESSE and kisses him on the cheek.)

JESSE: Is the Son of God betrayed with a kiss?!

    (JUDAS, greatly upset and shaken, turns and runs away)

EXT. JUDAS' OFFICE. NIGHT.

    (Sound of sirens. NO DIALOGUE.)

STUDY SCENE:
NO. 18

The scene between Jesse and Peter is most important as Jesse has little time left to help Peter understand the series of events that are about to take place. At the same time, Peter is sensing the need to be with Jesse. His desire is to follow God, no matter what, and Jesse has always taken the time to explain things to Peter that he didn't know or understand.

1. When Peter says to Jesse; "Something's wrong", what is Jesse relating to Peter in the following statements:

A. "For many, with whom I've come into contact, my cause is lost".

> *Mark 4:14-20* **"The sower sows the word. These are the ones on the path where the word is sown: when they hear, Satan immediately comes and takes away the word that is sown in them. And these are the ones sown on rocky ground: when they hear the word, they immediately receive it with joy. <u>But they have no root, and endure only for a while; then, when trouble or persecution arises on account of the word, immediately they fall away</u>. And others are those sown among the thorns: these are the ones who hear the word, but the cares of the world, and the lure of wealth, and the desire for other things come in and choke the word, and it yields nothing. And these are the ones sown on the good soil: they hear the word and accept it and bear fruit, thirty and sixty and a hundredfold."**

B. "Even those of you who I've gathered around me as a nucleus to carry on the truths that I've taught you, half believe and half doubt."

*John 14:5-11   Thomas said to Him, "Lord, we do not know where You are going. How can we know the way?" Jesus said to him, **"I am the way, and the truth, and the life. No one comes to the Father except through Me. If you know Me, you will know My Father also. From now on you do know Him and have seen Him."** Philip said to Him, "Lord, show us the Father, and we will be satisfied." Jesus said to him, **"Have I been with you all this time, Philip, <u>and you still do not know Me?</u> Whoever has seen Me has seen the Father. How can you say, 'Show us the Father'? Do you not believe that I am in the Father and the   Father is in Me? The words that I say to you I do not speak on My own; but the Father who dwells in Me does His works. Believe Me that I am in the Father and the Father is in Me; but if you do not, then believe Me because of the works themselves."***

C. "In spite of all that I've taught you, tonight you'll all forsake me, because you'll think I've failed, because I choose not to use material force to overcome my enemies."

*John 16:32-33   **"The hour is coming, indeed it has come, when you will be scattered, each one to his home, and you will leave Me alone. Yet I am not alone because the Father is with Me. I have said this to you, so that in Me you may have peace. In the world you face persecution. But take courage; I have conquered the world!"***

*Matt. 26:31   Then Jesus said to them, **"You will all become deserters because of Me this night; for it is written, 'I will strike the shepherd, and the sheep of the flock will be scattered.'"***

2. Peter promises total devotion and commitment to Jesse. He's quite sure he 'll never fail him.

A. "Jesse, I'll never forsake you. I know who you are, and nobody 's gonna get to you unless they come through me first, NOBODY."

> *Mark 14:29   Peter said toHim, "Even though all become deserters, I will not."*

> *Matt. 26:33   Peter said to Him, "Though all become deserters because of You, I will never desert You."*

> *John 13:37   Peter said to Him, "Lord, why can I not follow You now? I will lay down my life for You."*

3. Jesse knows what is about to take place and is aware of Peter's weakness, He has little time to plant the following seeds in Peter that will take root ... spiritually nurture him ... and bring about a strong harvest.

A. "I know your heart is in the right place, but before you can be the rock that I've called you to be, you must overcome your greatest weakness, Peter, and that's fear."

> *John 13:38   Jesus answered, **"Will you lay down your life for Me? Very truly, I tell you, before the cock crows, you will have denied Me three times."***

B. "Tonight, Satan will sift you and before the night is over, you'll deny knowing me three times."

> *Luke 22:31, 33-34   **"Simon, Simon, listen! Satan has demanded to sift all of you like wheat."** And he said to Him "Lord, I am ready to go with you to prison and to death!" Jesus said, **"I tell you, Peter, the cock will not crow this day, until you have denied three times that you know Me."***

C. "The rest is up to the depth of your belief in the faith that you have in me. After tonight you must learn to walk by faith alone. A final test must come to all who walk by faith. You must rely on me alone. Trust in no other and seek no other help."

> *2Cor.5:7... for we walk by faith, not by sight.*

> *Hebr. 11:17 By faith Abraham, when put to the test, offered up Isaac. He who had received the promises was ready to offer up his only son, ...*

> *Matt. 4:4 **"A Man shall not live on bread alone, but on every word that proceeds out of the mouth of God."***

> *Hebr. 11:6 And without faith it is impossible to please God, for whoever would approach Him must believe that He exists and that He rewards those who seek Him.*

D. "Expect storms if you're to do my work. Because of your love, friendship and bond to do my work, you'll excite the enemy the malice and hatred of all those who are not on my side."

> *John 15:18-19 **"If the world hates you, be aware that it hated Me before it hated you. If you be-longed to the world, the world would love you as its own. Because you do not belong to the world, but I have chosen you out of the world; therefore, the world hates you."***

> *John 16:1-3 **"I have said these things to you to keep you from stumbling. They will put you out of the synagogues. Indeed, an hour is coming when those who kill you will think that by doing so they are offering service to God.   And they***

will do this because they have not known the Father or Me."

Matt. 10:16-22 "See, I am sending you out like sheep into the midst of wolves; so be wise as serpents and innocent as doves. Beware of them, for they will hand you over to councils and flog you in their synagogues;   and you will be dragged before governors and kings because of Me, as a testimony to them and the Gentiles. When they hand you over, do not worry about how you are to speak or what you are to say; for what you are to say will be given to you at that time;   for it is not you who speak, but the Spirit of your Father speaking through you. Brother will betray brother to death, and a father his child, and children will rise against parents and have them put to death;   and you will be hated by all because of My name. But the one who endures to the end will be saved."

E. "The enemy attacks the fortress... the stronghold, never the desert waste."

Prov. 21:22 A wise man scales the city of the mighty, and brings down the stronghold in which they trust.

Mark 3:27 "But no one can enter a strong man's house and plunder his property without first tying up the strong man; then indeed the house can be plundered."

F. "The group looks to you, so trust in the Spirit that I will send you ... not what you see, or what your present circumstances dictate."

John 14:26   "But the Advocate, the Holy Spirit, whom the Father will send in My name, will teach you everything, and remind you of all that I have said to you."

John 15:26-27 "When the Advocate comes, whom I will send to you from the Father, the Spirit of truth who comes from the Father, He will testify on My behalf. You also are to testify because you have been with Me from the beginning."

John 16:6-13 "__But because I have said these__ __things to you, sorrow has filled your hearts.__ *Nevertheless I tell you the truth: it is to your advantage that I go away, for if I do not go away, the Advocate will not come to you; but if I go, I will send Him to you. And when He comes, He will prove the world wrong about sin and righteousness and judgment: about sin, because they do not believe in Me; about righteousness, because I am going to the Father and you will see Me no longer; about judgment, because the ruler of this world has been condemned. "I still have many things to say to you, but you cannot bear them now. When the Spirit of truth comes, He will guide you into all the truth; for He will not speak on His own, but will speak whatever He hears, and He will declare to you the things that are to come."*

G. "If you truly love me, you'll survive and carry my message."

Luke 22:32.... "but I have prayed for you that your own faith may not fail; and you, when once __you have turned back,__ strengthen your brothers."

Mark 16:15 And He said to them, "Go into all the world and proclaim the good news to the whole creation.

4. What is the significance of armed men surrounding Jesse and who do they represent?

> *Mark 14: 43-44   Immediately, while He was still speaking, Judas, one of the twelve, arrived; and with him there was a crowd with swords and clubs, from the chief priests, the scribes, and the elders. Now the betrayer had given them a sign, saying, "The one I will kiss is the man; arrest Him and lead Him away under guard."*

5. When Judas walks up to Jesse, screams WHY!!!, ... what is immediately put into motion?

> *Mark 14:45   So when he came, he went up to Him at once and said, "Rabbi!" and kissed Him.*

6. What was possibly behind the look and hug that Jesse gave Judas?

> *Matt. 5:44   **"But I say to you, Love your enemies and pray for those who persecute you."***
>
> *Prov. 27:19   As in water face reflects face, so the heart of man reflects man.*

7. What was Jesse's final response to Judas?

> *Luke 22:48 ... but Jesus said to him, **"Judas, is it with a kiss that you are betraying the Son of Man?"***

NOTES:

INT. JUDAS' OFFICE. NIGHT: (SCENE 19)

	(JUDAS enters and finds JACKSON inside.)
JUDAS:	(OS) How the hell did you get (IN FRAME) in here, Jackson?
JACKSON:	I'm not a thief ... and I don't deal in deception. However, I do kill people.
JUDAS:	Is that why you're here?
JACKSON:	I wish it were that simple.
JUDAS:	What the hell are you talking about?
JACKSON:	Hell! That's what I'm talking about.
	(OS) That's a place you and I are gonna see a lot of.
	(IN FRAME) I never believed in hell, or heaven or God or anything ... until a few days ago. All I had to do was pull the trigger. I couldn't move my fingers I KNOW .. who he is.
	(OS) They're gonna kill him ...
	(IN FRAME) and there's not a damn thing I can do about it.
JUDAS:	Who's gonna kill who?
JACKSON:	(OS) JESSE.

INT. JUDAS' OFFICE. NIGHT (CONT'D):

JACKSON (CONT'D): (IN FRAME) ... And you

(OS)... You set him up.

JUDAS: I didn't set him up. I didn't set anybody
                          up, see? I gave him a little bit of a push
                          that's all, just so he'd accept
                          Cunningham's offer.

                          (OS) And I wanted him to take over

                          (IN FRAME) what was already his.
                          Now, can you imagine a world with that
                          kind of power, you know ... no war, no
                          hunger, no famine. Anyway,
                          Cunningham's not gonna kill Jesse, he
                          needs him ... you heard him say it
                          yourself.

JACKSON: Ponerous wants him dead, not
                          Cunningham. Cunningham will keep
                          him alive as long as he feels there's a
                          chance Jesse will join him. If Ponerous
                          convinces him otherwise, it's over.

JUDAS: You're a liar! You're a liar!

JACKSON: (OS) Are you an idiot?

                          (IN FRAME) ... or just plain stupid?
                          Your little fiasco on the beach probably
                          assured Jesse he'll never live to see
                          tomorrow night!! And as for me,
                          it's my guess DeCARMO and I will
                          both be hit. So, why? ... why should I

INT. JUDAS' OFFICE. NIGHT (CONT'D):

JACKSON (CONT'D): lie to you? I really came here to ask you a question.

(OS) How can anyone live with a man like Jesse for so long and willfully betray him? ... because he's not what you wanted him to be? I hated you before. I don't now ... I just feel sorry for you.

(JACKSON exits.)

JUDAS: Jackson. It wasn't about money ... not for thirty pieces of silver.

STUDY SCENE:
NO. 19

Asa has already informed Judas that Jackson has become a problem and has asked Judas to notify her, immediately, if he sees Jackson. When Judas enters his office he doesn't seem really surprised to find Jackson there playing with silvers bars. Jackson hasn't come to steal Judas' blood money; nor, to kill Judas. Killing Judas would be a simple matter for Jackson as that's what he does as a profession. He isn't pretending to be something that he isn't, as he seemingly feels Judas is. Jackson is convinced that both he and Judas are on a fast track headed for hell (A place of eternal torment) and both deserve to be there. He came to tell him that Jesse's going to be killed, because he, Judas, had set him up.

Judas is convinced Jackson is lying and outright calls him a liar. Jackson knows that both he and DeCarmo will be executed and has no reason to lie to anyone. He feels totally powerless to prevent Jesse's death and tells Judas that his little fiasco on the beach, the other night, has sealed Jesse's fate ... and it's Ponerous who's out to kill Jesse. Because of his connection with Cunningham, Jackson knew exactly what Judas had done and for what price. Jackson had to know what kind of a man would betray the Son of God, so he asks Judas:

"How can anyone live with a man like Jesse for so long and willfully betray him, because he's not what you wanted him to be? I hated you before, I don't now ... I just feel sorry for you."

As Jackson exits the office, Judas speaks ... but only to himself: "Jackson, it wasn't about money ... not for thirty pieces of silver."

In this scene Judas is trying to convince Jackson and himself, that he did the right thing. Even if Judas was to succeed in pushing Jesse to use his power to end hunger, famine and war, it could only result in bringing the battle itself to a halt ... but not the cause.

Distrust and hatred sets into motion the chain reaction of war and evil that man inflicts upon mankind. If we are to end the pain and suffering we must learn to counter hate with love, fear with trust. The outcome of any battle is never truly decided on the battlefield, rather, won or lost in our hearts. God has never forced His Will for our life on any of us, rather, He has given us the freedom of choosing to live in Him, or die in our own sin. Judas had the same freedom.

It is a fact that Judas was hand picked by Jesus as one of the 12 disciples. Jesus sent the 12 out in pairs to minister in His name. This means that even though Jesus knew that Judas was to betray Him, He still gave, to Judas, the same authority to minister to the sick, raise the dead, cast out demons, etc., as he gave to the other 11 disciples.

> *Mark 6:7 And He summoned the twelve and began to send them out in pairs; and He was giving them authority over the unclean spirits;*
>
> *Matt. 10:1-15 And having summoned His twelve disciples, He gave them authority over unclean spirits, to cast them out, and to heal every kind of disease and every kind of sickness. Now the names of the twelve apostles are these: The first, Simon, who is called Peter, and Andrew his brother; and James the {son} of Zebedee, and John his brother; Philip and Bartholomew; Thomas and Matthew the tax-gatherer; James the {son} of Alphaeus, and Thaddaeus; Simon the Zealot, and Judas Iscariot, the one who betrayed Him. These twelve Jesus sent out after instructing them, saying, "Do not go in {the} way of {the} Gentiles, and do not enter {any} city of the Samaritans; but rather go to the lost sheep of the house of Israel. "And as you go, preach, saying, 'The kingdom of heaven is at hand.' "Heal {the} sick, raise {the} dead, cleanse {the} lepers, cast out demons; freely you received, freely give.*

> *"Do not acquire gold, or silver, or copper for your money belts, or a bag for {your} journey, or even two tunics, or sandals, or a staff; for the worker is worthy of his support. And into whatever city or village you enter, inquire who is worthy in it; and abide there until you go away. And as you enter the house, give it your greeting. And if the house is worthy, let your {greeting of} peace come upon it; but if it is not worthy, let your {greeting of} peace return to you. And whoever does not receive you, nor heed your words, as you go out of that house or that city, shake off the dust of your feet. Truly I say to you, it will be more tolerable for {the} land of Sodom and Gomorrah in the day of judgment, than for that city"*

1. Why then did Judas betray Jesus? Did he betray Him because;

   A. As a Zealot he wanted Jesus to establish His Kindgom on Earth?

   B. Of greed... for thirty pieces of silver?

   C. It was predestined?

> *John 6:64-71* **"But there are some of you who do not believe."** *For Jesus knew from the beginning who they were who did not believe, and who it was that would betray Him. And He was saying,* <u>**"For this reason I have said to you, that no one can come to Me, unless it has been granted him from the Father."**</u> *As a result of this many of His disciples withdrew, and were not walking with Him anymore. Jesus said therefore to the twelve,* **"You do not want to go away also, do you?"** *Simon Peter answered Him, "Lord, to whom shall we go? You have words of eternal life. And we have believed and have come to know that You are the Holy One of God."*

*Jesus   answered them, **"Did I Myself not choose you, the twelve, and {yet} one of you is a devil?"** Now He meant Judas {the son} of Simon Iscariot, for he, one of the twelve, was going to betray Him.*

*Matt. 26:20-25 Now when evening had come, He was reclining {at the table} with the twelve disciples. And as they were eating, He said, **"Truly I say to you that one of you will betray Me."** And being deeply grieved, they each one began to say to Him, "Surely not I, Lord?" And He answered and said, **"He who dipped his hand with Me in the bowl is the one who will betray Me.   The Son of Man {is to} go, just as it is written of Him; but woe to that man by whom the Son of Man is betrayed!** <u>**It would have been good for that man if he had not been born**</u>**."** And Judas, who was betraying Him, answered and said, "Surely it is not I, Rabbi?" He said to him, **"You have said {it} yourself."***

Luke 22:2-6 And the chief priests and the scribes were seeking how they might put Him to death; for they were afraid of the people. <u>And Satan entered into Judas</u> who was called Iscariot, belonging to the number of the twelve. And he went away and discussed with the chief priests and officers how he might betray Him to them. And they were glad, and agreed to give him money. And he <u>consented,</u> and {began} <u>seeking a good opportunity to betray Him to them apart from the multitude</u>.

*John 17:12   **"While I was with them, I was keeping them in Thy name which Thou hast given Me; and I guarded them, <u>and not one of them perished but the son of perdition, that the Scripture might be fulfilled</u>"***

Acts 1:16   Brethren, the Scripture had to be fulfilled, which the Holy Spirit foretold by the mouth of David concerning Judas, who became a guide to those who arrested Jesus.

NOTES:

EXT. CUNNINGHAM'S HOME. DAY: (SCENE 20)

(SONG **THIRTY PIECES OF
SILVER**" PLAYS OVER ENTIRE
SCENE)

(JUDAS drives up in van.)

SONG LYRICS: SOME PEOPLE HAVE ... SOME
PEOPLE DON'T
SOME PEOPLE WILL ... AND SOME
PEOPLE WON'T

WELL, IT'S ABOUT THE SAME ... ALL
OVER THE WORLD
HOW CAN WE SURVIVE WITHOUT
MONEY, MONEY, MONEY, MONEY,
MONEY, MONEY, MONEY

(JUDAS throws the briefcase, full of silver, and SMASHES IT against steps of
CUNNINGHAM'S HOME. He drives
off. We follow him down the highway.)

EXT. HIGHWAY. DAY:

SONG LYRICS: IT'S COLD IN THE STREETS
WHEN YOU'VE GOT TO COMPETE
WITH EACH OTHER

YOU FEEL YOU'VE GOT TO CHEAT
AND STEAL
IF YOU'RE GONNA SURVIVE ONE
ANOTHER

YOU SAY THE WORLD IS LIKE A
GUN
WITH EVERYONE FIGHTING FOR
THE TRIGGER

EXT. HIGHWAY. DAY (CONT'D):

SONG LYRICS:	JUST TO KILL ANOTHER MAN FOR THIRTY PIECES OF SILVER
	YESTERDAY A MAN WAS CRUCIFIED
CHORUS:	(FOR THIRTY PIECES OF SILVER)
SONG LYRICS:	AND TODAY ANOTHER MAN IS GONNA DIE
CHORUS:	(FOR THIRTY PIECES OF SILVER)
SONG LYRICS:	WHAT FOR?
CHORUS:	(FOR THIRTY PIECES OF SILVER)
SONG LYRICS:	I SAID, WHAT FOR?
CHORUS:	(FOR THIRTY PIECES OF SILVER, SILVER, SILVER)

EXT. BEACH. DAY:

	(JUDAS drives to the beach and gets out of the van)
SONG LYRICS:	WHOEVER SAID YOU GOTTA DIE TO GO TO HELL IN THE GHETTO
	THERE'S A LOT OF LOVE AROUND BUT YOU THINK IT'S ONLY FOUND ... IN A BORDELLO
	I SAID IF YOU'VE GOT THE BREAD YOU CAN ALWAYS FIND A MAN TO DELIVER

EXT. BEACH. DAY: (CONT'D)

SONG LYRICS:	ANYTHING YOU WANT
CHORUS:	(FOR THIRTY PIECES OF SILVER)
SONG LYRICS:	I SAID ANYTHING YOU WANT
CHORUS:	(FOR THIRTY PIECES OF SILVER, SILVER, SILVER)
SONG LYRICS:	YOU COULD LOSE YOUR "S O U L"

STUDY SCENE:
NO. 20

In this scene it's obvious Judas is in turmoil and facing a desperate situation. He has been told by Jackson that Jesse is going to die... and that only Ponerous can stop it. Judas, in a desperate attempt to put an end to it, returns with the briefcase containing silver bars. The "gate" is closed and he can not enter. He contemplates for a while, and throws the briefcase over the gate. On impact, the briefcase spills its contents on the steps. He takes off, trying to locate the others, but it looks as if it's too late.

Matt. 27:1-10 Now when morning had come, all the chief priests and the elders of the people took counsel against Jesus to put Him to death; and they bound Him, and led Him away, and delivered Him up to Pilate the governor. Then when Judas, who had betrayed Him, saw that He had been condemned, he felt remorse and returned the thirty pieces of silver to the chief priests and elders, saying, "I have sinned by betraying innocent blood." But they said, "What is that to us? See {to that} yourself!" And he threw the pieces of silver into the sanctuary and departed; and he went away and hanged himself. And the chief priests took the pieces of silver and said, "It is not lawful to put them into the temple treasury, since it is the price of blood." And they counseled together and with the money bought the Potter's Field as a burial place for strangers. For this reason that field has been called the Field of Blood to this day. Then that which was spoken through Jeremiah the prophet was fulfilled, saying, "AND THEY TOOK THE THIRTY PIECES OF SILVER, THE PRICE OF THE ONE WHOSE PRICE HAD BEEN SET by the sons of Israel; AND THEY GAVE THEM FOR THE POTTER'S FIELD, AS THE LORD DIRECTED ME."

This would be a good time to "carefully and prayerfully" go over the lyrics of the song... **"Thirty Pieces of Silver"**, and study its <u>entire</u> message, as it relates to the ills of worldliness and its cost.

Phil. 2:21   For they all seek after their own interests, not those of Christ Jesus.

Luke 3:14   Do not take money from anyone by force, or accuse {anyone} falsely, and be content with your wages.

Phil. 4:11-13 Not that I speak from want; for I have learned to be content in whatever circumstances I am.   I know how to get along with humble means, and I also know how to live in prosperity; in any and every circumstance I have learned the secret of being filled and going hungry, both of having abundance and suffering need. I can do all things through Him who strengthens me.

1Tim. 6:6-11 But godliness {actually} is a means of great gain, when accompanied by contentment. For we have brought nothing into the world, so we can not take anything out of it either.   And if we have food and covering, with these we shall be content. But those who want to get rich fall into temptation and a snare and many foolish and harmful desires which plunge men into ruin and destruction. For the love of money is a root of all sorts of evil, and some by longing for it have wandered away from the faith, and pierced themselves with many a pang. But flee from these things, you man of God; and pursue righteousness, godliness, faith, love, perseverance {and} gentleness.

Hebr. 13:5 Let your character be free from the love of money, being content with what you have; for He Himself has said, "I WILL NEVER DESERT YOU,

NOR WILL I EVER FORSAKE YOU,"

Gal. 6:7-8 Do not be deceived, God is not mocked; for whatever a man sows, this he will also reap. For the one who sows to his own flesh shall from the flesh reap corruption, but the one who sows to the Spirit shall from the Spirit reap eternal life.

Rom. 8:5-8 For those who are according to the flesh set their minds on the things of the flesh, but those who are according to the Spirit, the things of the Spirit. For the mind set on the flesh is death, but the mind set on the Spirit is life and peace, because the mind set on the flesh is hostile toward God; for it does not subject itself to the law of God, for it is not even able {to do so} ; and those who are in the flesh cannot please God.

*Mark 8:36-37 **"For what does it profit a man to gain the whole world, and forfeit his soul? For what shall a man give in exchange for his soul?"***

There is nothing on the face of this earth worth our being separated from God. No matter how much we may desire something; ie; social position, promotion, houses, cars, etc.; None of them are worth it if received at the price of someone else's life or well being.

None of us are immune to making mistakes. The further we stray from what is honest and pure and Godly, the harder it will be to find our way back ... as our heart becomes harder and harder. The only one that can pierce that hard heart and cleanse it is God Almighty through the blood of Jesus. When we acknowledge our mistakes, <u>repent</u> for those mistakes and ask God for His forgiveness, we <u>will be forgiven</u>. We do not have to end up like Judas.

James 4:7-8   Submit therefore to God. Resist the devil and he will flee from you.   Draw near to God and He will draw near to you.

NOTE:

EXT. ABANDONED BOATHOUSE. DAY   (SCENE 21)

(HENCHMAN beats up JESSE.)

HENCHMAN: Unh   (as he strikes JESSE.)

JESSE: AHH!

HENCHMAN: Unh   (strikes him again.)

JESSE: Oh ahh! ahh!

CUNNINGHAM: That's enough!

JESSE: Moans

CUNNINGHAM: We've been at this a long time. Why won't you defend yourself?

JESSE: Ohoo!

CUNNINGHAM: If you won't help me, then you must be out to destroy me.

JESSE: I seek to destroy no one. You're free to choose your own destiny.

CUNNINGHAM: That's encouraging. You finally decided to say something. Now, Why does Ponerous want to destroy you?

JESSE: I came into this world to bear witness of the truth ... to be the bridge between God and man for anyone to cross who would know and believe in me. Only those who seek the truth will hear my voice and cross the bridge. Ponerous

EXT. ABANDONED BOATHOUSE. DAY (CONT'D):

JESSE (CONT'D):   seeks to destroy the truth,

                    (OS) rather than embrace it.

CUNNINGHAM: (OS) Are you again claiming to be the Son of God?

JESSE: I am the Son of God!

CUNNINGHAM: Don't you realize that I and only I have the power to save or destroy you?

JESSE: The, only

                    (OS) power you have is that which my Father has allowed you to have.

CUNNINGHAM: (OS) Who is your Father?

JESSE: (OS) If you can see me

                    (IN FRAME) and don't know who I am, even though I've told you, then how could you know my Father if you can't see Him?

CUNNINGHAM: (Speaking to Ponerous) If you want him dead, you kill him. I want no part of it.

PONEROUS: Looks like I win. Doesn't look like your Father will save you, or can save you.

                    (OS) I guess, um, since we weren't struck down, I personally

                    (IN FRAME) am gonna see that ... your teachings die here ... with you.

EXT. ABANDONED BOATHOUSE. DAY (CONT'D):

PONEROUS (CONT'D):   (OS) Bring the big one to me.

(HENCHMEN bring PETER forward.)

(OS) Aren't you the

(IN FRAME) spokesman for that pathetic group of degenerates?

PETER: I don't know what you're talking about.

PONEROUS: (OS) I'm sure you know Jesse, here.

PETER: (OS) I've never seen him before this day!

PONEROUS: (OS) Look at him, you blubbering fool!

PETER: Damn you, Ponerous! I told you, I'VE NEVER SEEN HIM BEFORE! (SCREAMS)

(OS) NEVER!!

PONEROUS: (OS) Oh, cut him loose. It's, obvious he's no threat to me. I wonder how long it will take your followers to forget about a man they'll never see again. I speak for God, and the people will continue to follow me.

JESSE: **You hypocrite**! You travel the world to find one convert, and when you do, you make him twice as much a **son of hell** as **yourself**!

EXT. ABANDONED BOATHOUSE. DAY (CONT'D):

PONEROUS: Hell - is, that what you said? That's exactly where I'm sending you.

JESSE: I know, and in three days I'll return with the keys.

PONEROUS: Hm, hm, hm, heh. That'll be your best trick yet. You know what to do with THEM. Use spikes

(OS) only on Jesse.

(IN FRAME) **Nail him!!!**

(HENCHMEN drag JESSE and others up the ramp to the boathouse. JAMES falls down and the HENCHMEN kick him.)

HENCHMEN: C'mon..   Get up! Let's go! Get up! Come on Wimp! Etc.

PONEROUS: (OS) They call you the Rose of Sharon a King sent of God.

(IN FRAME) What is a rose without thorns? A King without a crown?

(Ponerous slams crown of thorns on Jesse's head)

JESSE: OUuAuhhhh!

PONEROUS: Ha, ha, ALL HAIL!, ha, ha, THE KING! Ha, ha,

EXT. ABANDONED BOATHOUSE. DAY (CONT'D):

> (Thunder claps. All cover their ears and duck.)

HENCHMEN: Ah!

STUDY SCENE:
NO. 21

As a result of a plot to kill Jesse and Judas' betrayal, a trial is in progress. Jesse's being beaten and we can see, by the stripes on his back, that he has been flogged.

> *John 19:1 Then Pilate took Jesus and had Him flogged.*

> *Matt. 26:67 Then they spat in His face and beat Him with their fists; and others slapped Him,*

1. It is apparent that Cunningham has been questioning Jesse for quite some time, and Jesse hasn't been answering any of the charges against him, or defending himself.

> *Matt. 27:13-14 Then Pilate said to Him, "Do You not hear how many things they testify against You?" And He did not answer him with regard to even a {single} charge, so that the governor was quite amazed.*

2. Cunningham, frustrated by not getting anywhere with Jesse, tries a different approach; "If you won't help me, then you must be out to destroy me." Jesse answers him:

A. "I seek to destroy no one. You're free to choose your own destiny."

> *Luke 9:56 **"for the Son of Man did not come to destroy men's lives, but to save them."***

> *Ezek. 18:23 "Do I have any pleasure in the death of the wicked," declares the Lord GOD, "rather than that he should turn from his ways and live?"*

Rom. 6:23   For the wages of sin is death, but the free gift of God is eternal life in Christ Jesus our Lord.

3. Relieved, Cunningham presses on: "Now, why does Ponerous want to destroy you?" Jesse responds:

A. "I came into this world to bear witness of the truth ...

*Luke 18:37   **"For this I was born, and for this I came into the world, to testify to the truth."***

B. ... to be the bridge between God and man for anyone to cross who would know and believe in me.

*John 14:6   Jesus said to him, **"I am the way, and the truth, and the life; no one comes to the Father, but through Me."***

C. ... Only those who seek the truth will hear my voice and cross the bridge.

*Luke 18:37 ... **"Everyone who belongs to the truth listens to my voice."***

D. ... Ponerous seeks to destroy the truth, rather than embrace it."

*Matt. 23:13   **"But woe to you, scribes and Pharisees, hypocrites, because you shut off the kingdom of heaven from men; for you do not enter in yourselves, nor do you allow those who are entering to go in."***

4. Cunningham has to get to the bottom of who Jesse is, so he asks him: "Are you again claiming to be the Son of God?" Jesse confirms: "I am the Son of God?"

Luke 23:3   And Pilate asked Him, saying, "Are You the King of the Jews?" And He answered him and said, " {It is as} you say."

*John 8:28   So Jesus said, **"When you have lifted up the Son of Man, then you will realize that I am He, and that I do nothing on My own, but I speak these things as the Father instructed Me."***

*Luke 22:70   And they all said, "Are You the Son of God, then?" And He said to them, **"Yes, I am."***

5. Cunningham feels that he is the only one who has the power to release or condemn Jesse, and forces the following exchange between them:

A. CUNNINGHAM: "Don't you realize that I and only I have the power to save or destroy you?"

John 19:10   "Do You not know that I have power to release You, and power to crucify You?"

B. JESSE: "The only power you have is that which my Father has allowed you to have."

*John 19:11   **"You would have no power over Me unless it had been given you from above."***

C. CUNNINGHAM: "Who is your father?"

John 8:19   And so they were saying to Him, "Where is Your Father?"

D. JESSE: "If you can see me and don't know who I am, even tho I've told you, then how could you know my Father if you can't see Him?"

> *John 8:19*   ***"You know neither Me nor My Father. If you knew Me, you would know My Father also."***
>
> *John 5:37*   ***"And the Father who sent Me, He has borne witness of Me. You have neither heard His voice at any time, nor seen His form.***

6. Totally exasperated, Cunningham turns the whole matter over to Ponerous as he can't find any reason good enough to order Jesse's death... much less crucify him. As if he is washing his hands of Jesse's blood, Cunningham tells Ponerous:

> A.   "If you want him dead, you kill him. I want no part of it."
>
> > *Luke 23:13-15   And Pilate summoned the chief priests and the rulers and the people, and said to them, "You brought this man to me as one who incites the people to rebellion, and behold, having examined Him before you, I have found no guilt in this Man regarding the charges which you make against Him. "No, nor has Herod, for he sent Him back to us; and behold, nothing deserving death has been done by Him."*
> >
> > *Matt. 27:24   And when Pilate saw that he was accomplishing nothing, ... he said "I am innocent of this Man's blood; see {to that} yourselves."*
> >
> > *John 19:16   Then he (Pilate) handed Him over to them to be crucified.*

7. Gloating, Ponerous starts into Jesse:

> A.   "Looks like I win. Doesn't look like your Father will save you, or can save you. I guess, um, since we weren't

struck down, I personally am gonna see that your teachings die here with you."

> *Matt. 27:41-43   In the same way the chief priests also, along with the scribes and elders, were mocking {Him,} and saying,   "He saved others; He can not save Himself. He is the King of Israel; let Him now come down from the cross, and we shall believe in Him.   "HE TRUSTS IN GOD; LET HIM DELIVER {Him} now, IF HE TAKES PLEASURE IN HIM; for He said, 'I am the Son of God.'"*

8. Full of himself, Ponerous yanks on Peter's beard forcing him to look at Jesse, and yells: "Look at him you blubbering fool!"

9. Peter responds (the third time):

A. "DAMN YOU Ponerous, I told you, I'VE NEVER SEEN HIM BEFORE! (SCREAMS) NEVER!!"

> *Matt. 26:74 Then he (Peter) <u>began to curse</u>, and he <u>swore an oath</u>, "I do not know the man!"*

10.   As Peter looked into Jesse's eyes, he met a look of understanding and compassion.

> *Luke 22:61   And the Lord turned and looked at Peter. And Peter remembered the word of the Lord, how He had told him, **"Before a cock crows today, you will deny Me three times."***

> *Luke 22:32   **"but I have prayed for you, that your faith may not fail; and you, when once you have turned again, strengthen your brothers."***

11. Still consumed by self righteousness, Ponerous goes out of his way saying: "I ... speak for God, and the people will continue to follow ... ME." Grabbing that hypocritical spirit by the throat... Jesse tells it like it is:

> A. "YOU HYPOCRITE!   You travel the world to find one convert, and when you do, you make him twice as much a **son of hell as yourself!**"
>
>> *Matt. 23:15   "Woe to you, scribes and Pharisees, hypocrites! For you cross sea and land to make a single convert, and you make the new convert <u>twice as much a son of hell</u> as yourselves."*

12. Ponerous does a cutsie play on the word "Hell" and tells Jesse: "that's exactly where I'm sending you!"   Already knowing the outcome... Jesse answers:

> A. "I know and in three days I will return with the keys.
>
>> *Matt. 20:19 "and will deliver Him to the Gentiles to mock and scourge and crucify {Him,} and on the third day He will be raised up."*
>
>> *Luke 9:22   "The Son of Man must suffer many things, and be rejected by the elders and chief priests and scribes, and be killed, and be raised up on the third day."*
>
>> *Rev. 1:17-18 And when I saw Him, I fell at His feet as a dead man. And He laid His right hand upon me, saying, "Do not be afraid; I am the first and the last, and the living One; and I was dead, and behold, I am alive forevermore, and <u>I have the keys of death and of Hades.</u>"*

13. Ponerous orders "spikes" to be used only on Jesse. Looking into Jesse's eyes, he issues a final command: "NAIL HIM!"

> *Acts 2:23 this {Man} , delivered up by the pre-determined plan and foreknowledge of God, you nailed to a cross by the hands of godless men and put {Him} to death.*

14. Ponerous, full of indignation, mocks Jesse referring to him as "The Rose of Sharon.... a King sent of God?"

> *Song 2:1 "I AM the rose of Sharon , The lily of the valleys. "* (other names for Christ ref. NASB Open Bible)

> *John 12:13 they took the branches of the palm trees, and went out to meet Him, and {began} to cry out, "Hosanna! BLESSED IS HE WHO COMES IN THE NAME OF THE LORD, even the King of Israel. "*

15. Ponerous just can't help himself and fashions out what he thinks to be ... a final insult:

    A. "What is a rose without thorns ... A King without a crown?"

    > *Matt. 27:29 .... and after twisting some thorns into a crown, they put it on His head.*

    B. "All Hail the King! ha, ha," etc.

    > *Matt. 27:29 ... and mocked Him, saying, "Hail, King of the Jews!"*

NOTES:

INT. ABANDONED BOATHOUSE. DAY: (SCENE 22)

PONEROUS: GET IT OVER WITH!

(HENCHMAN hoists JESSE up to crucify him.)

JOHN: Lord!!!

JESSE: Ah...ugh...ugh...oh! (OS) Ah! Ah! Ah! Oh!

(HENCHMEN climb ladder and drive nails through his hands.)

Aaaahhh! Oh oh. Aaaaahhh! Ah Ah. FATHER!! Forgive them! Ohh...Ohh.

(HENCHMEN drive nails through his feet.)

(OS) Ahhh!! (IN FRAME) They don't know what they're doing!!

(OS) Ahhh!! Oh... Oh.
(IN FRAME) (Breath comes in gasps)

JACKSON: (OS) JESSE!! (IN FRAME) JESSE! Take me with you!

JESSE: (OS) This day   (IN FRAME) you will be with me in Paradise.

(CLOUD covers boathouse. Thunder rolls and claps. Lightening strikes all around the group.)

GROUP: Ohh, No! Ah! Get out here! Go! Oh, my God! Help me Man! Go! Ah! Etc.

INT. ABANDONED BOATHOUSE. DAY (CONT'D):

PONEROUS: You three, stay here! Make sure he dies!

EXT. WOODS. DAY:

                       (HENCHMEN burst through the bushes, running. Ponerous follows along. All are running. Peter runs and collapses.)

PONEROUS: Uh...uh

HENCHMEN: Uh.. uh.. oh. Etc.

INT. ABANDONED BOATHOUSE. DAY:

JESSE: Ohh... **FATHER!**, . Into Thy hands, I commit my spirit. Ahh! Ahhh!

EXT. WOODS. DAY:

JESSE: (VO) It is finished!

                       (LIGHTNING strikes tree... Concussion knocks PONEROUS to the ground)

PONEROUS: AHHHH!

INT. ABANDONED BOATHOUSE. DAY:

                       (JESSE takes a DYING GASP and his spirit leaves his body and descends into the ground.)

EXT. WOODS. DAY:

                       (Thunder and lightening strike out and chase Ponerous.)

EXT. WOODS. DAY (CONT'D):

PONEROUS: Ah! Ugh! (PONEROUS runs off.)

INT. ABANDONED BOATHOUSE. DAY:

(HENCHMAN climbs up ladder to JESSE, drives a spear through JESSE's side. Lightning knocks HENCHMAN off ladder.)

HENCHMAN: Ah!

EXT. WOODS. DAY:

(PONEROUS runs, lightning and storm chases him.)

PONEROUS: Ah!

(PONEROUS comes upon an abandoned Temple. Pulls at gates.)

Please! Is anyone in there? PLEASE!

(PONEROUS runs and is pushed into the building by lightning. He falls stumbles through the door and falls inside a mausoleum.)

STUDY SCENE:
NO. 22

This is the most, difficult and painful scene in the film to watch, as it represents the "VISUAL COMMUNION" between God, Jesus and each one of us. It also represents the cup Jesus had to drink, over which He had agonized and, while in fervent prayer, shed great drops of blood at Gethsemane. By partaking of this cup He, who was without sin, took upon Himself all sin, past, present and future, and sin was crucified on the cross with Him. Jesus became the sacrificial lamb, the final atonement of sin for all mankind. When His purpose on earth was accomplished and scripture fulfilled, He cried out; "It is Finished".

Only through His eyes could we ever see and begin to understand His pain, suffering, and the depth of His love for us. Beyond the agony of nails piercing flesh and His blood being shed, He faced and endured separation from His Father. God could not look upon sin; therefore, He had to turn His back on His only Son. As Jesus hung on the cross griped by utter desolation; He cried out: "My God, My God, why hast Thou forsaken Me?"

As the nails are being driven through His hands and feet, we again see the "VISUAL COMMUNION" ... "the establishment of the new covenant" by His body being given and His blood being poured out for us. Even during this darkest moment, Jesus intercedes on our behalf; "Father, forgive them for they know not what they do".

When the dying thief realized that forgiveness was assessable to him as well, he asked Jesus to remember him when He comes into His Kingdom. Jesus responded: "Truly I tell you, today you will be with Me in paradise".

In life, Jesus was totally committed to the will of His Father. Even with His last breath He entrusted His Spirit to Him: "Father, into Thy hands I commit My Spirit".

The "VISUAL COMMUNION" of Jesus' body being broken for us and His precious blood shed for our iniquities represents the greatest love story the world has ever known.

> *John 3:16* **"For God so loved the world that He gave (sacrificed) His only begotten Son, that who ever believes in Him should not perish but have eternal life."**

It is in the Garden of Gethsemane that this cup is passed from God to Jesus. When Jesus made the decision to drink of the cup, He knew full well what the cost would be.

1. The "Cup" At Gethsemane:

> *Matt. 26:38-39   Then He said to them,* **"My soul is deeply grieved, to the point of death; remain here and keep watch with Me."** *And He went a little beyond {them,} and fell on His face and prayed, saying,* **"My Father, if it is possible, let this cup pass from Me; yet not as I will, but as Thou wilt."**
>
> *Matt. 26:42   He went away again a second time and prayed, saying,* **"My Father, if this can not pass away unless I drink it, Thy will be done."**

2. Sweating Drops Of Blood:

> *Luke 22:43-44   Now an angel from heaven appeared to Him, strengthening Him. And being in agony He was praying very fervently; and His sweat became like drops of blood, falling down upon the ground.*

3. Took Sin Upon Himself That We Might Live:

> *1Pet. 3:18   For Christ also died for sins once for all, {the} just for {the} unjust, in order that He might bring us to God, having been put to death in the flesh, but made alive in the spirit;*

> *2Cor. 5:21   He made Him who knew no sin {to be} sin on our behalf, that we might become the righteousness of God in Him.*

> *1Pet. 2:24   and He Himself bore our sins in His body on the cross, that we might die to sin and live to righteousness; for by His wounds you were healed.*

4. Became The Sacrificial Lamb / Final Atonement:

> *Isa. 53:6-7   All of us like sheep have gone astray, Each of us has turned to his own way; But the LORD has caused the iniquity of us all To fall on Him.   He was oppressed and He was afflicted, Yet He did not open His mouth; Like a lamb that is led to slaughter,*

> *Heb. 7:26-27   For it was fitting that we should have such a high priest, holy, innocent, undefiled, separated from sinners and exalted above the heavens; who does not need daily, like those high priests, to offer up sacrifices, first for His own sins, and then for the {sins} of the people, because this He did once for all when He offered up Himself.*

> *Rom. 5:6,8 For while we were still helpless, at the right time Christ died for the ungodly.   But God demonstrates His own love toward us, in that while we were yet sinners, Christ died for us.*

> *John 1:29*   *"Behold, the Lamb of God who takes away the sin of the world!"*

5. My God, Why Has Thou Forsaken Me?

> *Ps. 22:1*   *My God, my God, why hast Thou forsaken me? Far from my deliverance are the words of my groaning.*

> *Mark 15:33-34*   *And when the sixth hour had come, <u>darkness fell over the whole land until the ninth hour.</u> And at the ninth hour Jesus cried out with a loud voice, "ELOI, ELOI, LAMA SABACHTHANI?" which is translated, "MY GOD, MY GOD, WHY HAST THOU FORSAKEN ME?"*

6. Nails Are Driven In His flesh / Prophesy Fulfilled: (Beginning of visual enactment / The Last Supper)

> *Zech. 12:10*   *"And I will pour out on the house of David and on the inhabitants of Jerusalem, the Spirit of grace and of supplication, so that they will look on Me whom they have pierced; and they will mourn for Him, as one mourns for an only son, and they will weep bitterly over Him, like the bitter weeping over a first-born."*

> *Acts 2:23*   *"this {Man} , delivered up by the predetermined plan and foreknowledge of God, you nailed to a cross by the hands of godless men and put {Him} to death."*

> *Isa. 53:5*   *"But He was pierced through for our transgressions, He was crushed for our iniquities; The chastening for our well-being {fell} upon Him, And by His scourging we are healed."*

7. Father Forgive Them:

> *Isa. 53:12   He poured out Himself to death, And was numbered with the transgressors; Yet He Himself bore the sin of many, And <u>interceded for the transgressors.</u>*

> *Luke 23:24   Then Jesus said, **"Father, forgive them; for they do not know what they are doing."***

8. The Dying Thief Asks Jesus To Remember him:

> *Luke 23:42-43   Then he (the thief) said, "Jesus, remember me when you come into your kingdom." Jesus replied, **"Truly I tell you, today you will be with me in Paradise."***

> *Hebr. 7:25   Hence, also, He is able to save forever those who draw near to God through Him, since He always lives to make intercession for them.*

9. Into Thy Hands I Commit My Spirit:

> *1Pet. 2:23   and while being reviled, He did not revile in return; while suffering, He uttered no threats, but kept entrusting {Himself} to Him who judges righteously;*

> *Luke 23:44-46 And it was now about the sixth hour, <u>and darkness fell over the whole land until the ninth hour,   the sun being obscured; and the veil of the temple was torn in two.</u> And Jesus, crying out with a loud voice, said, **"Father, INTO THY HANDS I COMMIT MY SPIRIT."***

10. It Is Finished: (Final visual enactment of the last supper)

A. <u>Importance of the Last Supper</u>: Eating the bread and drinking the wine symbolizes His blood of the covenant, the covering (forgiveness) of sin and the proclaiming of the Lord's death until He comes.

> *Matt. 26:26-28 Jesus took {some} bread, and after a blessing, He broke {it} and gave {it} to the disciples, and said,* **<u>"Take, eat; this is My body."</u>** *And when He had taken a cup and given thanks, He gave {it} to them, saying,* **"Drink from it, all of you; <u>for this is My blood of the covenant, which is poured out for many for forgiveness of sins."</u>**

> *1Cor. 11:24-28 and when He had given thanks, He broke it, and said,* **<u>"This is My body, which is for you; do this in remembrance of Me."</u>** *In the same way {He took} the cup also, after supper, saying,* **<u>"This cup is the new covenant in My blood; do this, as often as you drink {it,} in remembrance of Me."</u>** *For as often as you <u>eat his bread and drink the cup</u>, <u>you proclaim the Lord's death until He comes</u>. Therefore whoever eats the bread or drinks the cup of the Lord in an unworthy manner, shall be guilty of the body and the blood of the Lord. <u>But let a man examine himself</u>, and so let him eat of the bread and drink of the cup.*

B. The Final Enactment:

> *John 19:30   He said,* **<u>"It is finished!"</u>** *And He bowed His head, and gave up His spirit.*

> *Matt. 27:50-51 And Jesus cried out again with a loud voice, and yielded up {His} spirit. And behold, the veil of the temple was torn in two from top to bottom, and the earth shook; and the rocks were split.*

11. None Of His Bones Are Broken:

Ps. 34:20   He keeps all his bones; Not one of them is broken.

John 19:32-33   The soldiers therefore came, and broke the legs of the first man, and of the other man who was crucified with Him; but coming to Jesus, when they saw that He was already dead, they did not break His legs;

John 19:35-36   And he who has seen has borne witness, and his witness is true; and he knows that he is telling the truth, so that you also may believe. For these things came to pass, that the Scripture might be fulfilled, "NOT A BONE OF HIM SHALL BE BROKEN."

12. His Side Is Pierced:

Zech. 12:10   "And I will pour out on the house of David and on the inhabitants of Jerusalem, the Spirit of grace and of supplication, so that they will look on Me whom they have pierced; and they will mourn for Him, as one mourns for an only son, and they will weep bitterly over Him, like the bitter weeping over a first-born".

John 19:34,37 but one of the soldiers pierced His side with a spear, and immediately there came out blood and water. And again another Scripture says, "THEY SHALL LOOK ON HIM WHOM THEY PIERCED."

13. The Disciples Scatter:

> *Matt. 26:31   Then Jesus said to them,* **"You will all fall away because of Me this night, for it is written, 'I WILL STRIKE DOWN THE SHEPHERD, _AND THE SHEEP OF THE FLOCK SHALL BE SCATTERED_.'"**

NOTES:

INT. TEMPLE. DAY: (STUDY SCENE #23)

PONEROUS: Ah! Oh! Oh! (Looks around... wha...)

                     (A dark cloud gathers over the Temple.)

GOD: (VO) You never knew Me.

                     (Tombs open up and spirits of buried
                     dead rise up to cloud.)

PONEROUS: Ah! Oh! Oh! Etc.

                     (PONEROUS is consumed by fire that
                     comes from the center of the massive
                     cloud.)

PONEROUS: (Engulfed in flames SCREAMS)
                     AHHHHHH!

INT. ABANDONED BOATHOUSE. DAY:

                     (JUDAS enters. Sees JESSE. Slowly
                     walks over to the cross)

                     (SONG: "**DID YOU EVER HEAR
                     THE STORY**" PLAYS OVER SCENE)

SONG LYRICS: (VO) DID YOU EVER HEAR THE
                     STORY
                     ABOUT A MAN WHO COULD WALK
                     ON WATER
                     WHOSE LIFE WAS ONE LOVE
                     STORY ... TILL THE END

                     DID YOU EVER HEAR THE STORY

INT. ABANDONED BOATHOUSE. DAY (CONT'D):

    (JUDAS reaches toward JESSE'S FEET but doesn't touch him)

SONG LYRICS: 'BOUT A FOOL'S LOVE FOR MONEY
HOW IT TOOK HIS LIFE
AND HUNG HIS SOUL TO DRY

    WELL AS I LOOK AROUND ME ... I SEE NOTHING'S REALLY CHANGED

EXT. BEACH NIGHT:

    (FLASHBACK.)

JUDAS: WHY??!!

SONG LYRICS: (VO) THE WORLD STILL HAS ITS LOVERS AND ITS FOOLS
AND I CAN'T HELP BUT WONDER .
WHY NO ONE EVER LEARNS
THAT THE ONLY PRICE FOR FREEDOM ... IS LOVE

    (JUDAS takes a length of rope from JESSE'S CROSS and walks away)

    DO YOU WANNA HEAR A STORY OF A WORLD LIVING TOGETHER, OR DO YOU WANNA HEAR A STORY OF HOW IT ENDS

STUDY SCENE
NO. 23

In the previous scene and as this scene begins. Ponerous' piousness is reduced to total panic and fear as he desperately seeks a place to hide. Stumbling through the grave yard he comes upon a temple in ruins ... a long forgotten place of worship, and is driven inside. To his further dismay he falls into an empty tomb. Looking around he finds himself surrounded by graves and being overshadowed by a dark cloud. As the earth begins to quake some of the graves open and spirits are released. God tells Ponerous: **"You never knew Me"**.

Ponerous represents a religious spirit so wrapped up in pride and spiritual blindness, that he (it) never acknowledges.... only ... separates himself from God.   In the end, Ponerous and the spirit he represents, is consumed by a pillar of fire.

1. Did God ever dwell in a cloud or pillar of fire?

> *Ex. 13:21   The LORD went in front of them in a pillar of cloud by day, to lead them along the way, and in a pillar of fire by night, to give them light, so that they might travel by day and by night.*

> *Ex. 24:16-17 And the glory of the LORD rested on Mount Sinai, and the cloud covered it for six days; and on the seventh day He called to Moses from the midst of the cloud.   And to the eyes of the sons of Israel the appearance of the glory of the LORD was like a consuming fire on the mountain top.*

2. What was in the storm?

> *Jer. 23:19-23   "Behold, the storm of the LORD has gone forth in wrath, Even a whirling tempest; It will swirl down on the head of the wicked.*

*The anger of the LORD will not turn back Until
He has performed and carried out the purposes of
His heart; In the last days you will clearly understand it. I did not send {these} prophets, But
they ran. I did not speak to them, But they prophesied. But if they had stood in My council, Then
they would have announced My words to My
people, And would have turned them back from
their evil way And from the evil of their deeds.
'Am I a God who is near,' declares the LORD,
'And not a God far off?'"*

*Jer. 23: 25-32 "I have heard what the prophets
have said who prophesy falsely in My name,
saying, 'I had a dream, I had a dream!' How
long? Is there {anything} in the hearts of the
prophets who prophesy falsehood, even {these}
prophets of the deception of their own heart, who
intend to make My people forget My name by their
dreams which they relate to one another, just as
their fathers forgot My name because of Baal?
The prophet who has a dream may relate {his}
dream, but let him who has My word speak My
word in truth. What does straw have {in common}
with grain?" declares the LORD. "Is not My
word like fire?" declares the LORD, "and like a
hammer which shatters a rock?" "Therefore
behold, I am against the prophets," declares the
LORD, "who steal My words from each other.
"Behold, I am against the prophets," declares the
LORD, "who use their tongues and declare, ' {The
Lord} declares.' "Behold, I am against those who
have prophesied false dreams," declares the
LORD, "and related them, and led My people
astray by their falsehoods and reckless boasting;
yet I did not send them or command them, nor do
they furnish this people the slightest benefit,"
declares the LORD.*

3. Ponerous tries to hide from God.

> *Is. 2:19   And {men} will go into caves of the*
> *rocks, And into holes of the ground Before the*
> *terror of the LORD , And before the splendor of*
> *His majesty, When He arises to make the earth*
> *tremble.*

> *Jer. 23: 24   "Can a man hide himself in hiding*
> *places, So I do not see him?" declares the LORD.*
> *Do I not fill the heavens and the earth?" declares*
> *the LORD.*

4. God states to Ponerous from the cloud: "You never knew me:"

> *Matt. 7: 19-23   **"Every tree that does not bear***
> ***good fruit is cut down and thrown into the fire.***
> ***"So then, you will know them by their fruits.***
> ***"Not everyone who says to Me, 'Lord, Lord,' will***
> ***enter the kingdom of heaven; but he who does the***
> ***will of My Father who is in heaven.** "Many will*
> *say to Me on that day, 'Lord, Lord, did we not*
> *prophesy in Your name, and in Your name cast out*
> *demons, and in Your name perform many*
> *miracles?' "And then I will declare to them, '**I***
> ***NEVER KNEW YOU; DEPART FROM ME, YOU***
> ***WHO PRACTICE LAWLESSNESS.'"***

5. The earth quakes, tombs are opened and spirits rise:

> *Matt. 27:51-52   And behold, the veil of the temple*
> *was torn in two from top to bottom, and the earth*
> *shook; and the rocks were split, and the tombs*
> *were opened; <u>and many bodies of the saints who</u>*
> *<u>had fallen asleep were raised</u>;*

Matt. 27:53   and coming out of the tombs after His resurrection they entered the holy city and appeared to many.

6.   What is the significance of Ponerous being consumed by a pillar of fire?

John 3:36   "He who believes in the Son has eternal life; <u>but he who does not obey the Son shall not see life, but the wrath of God abides on him"</u>

Jer. 23:19-20   "<u>Behold, the storm of the LORD has gone forth in wrath, Even a whirling tempest; It will swirl down on the head of the wicked.</u> "The anger of the LORD will not turn back Until He has performed and carried out the purposes of His heart; In the last days you will clearly understand it."

Lev. 10:2   <u>And fire came out from the presence of the LORD and consumed them</u>, and they died before the LORD.

Heb . 12:29   for indeed God is a <u>consuming fire.</u>

There is not a lot known about the exact time of Judas' death. In this scene we see him entering the place of crucifixion <u>before</u> he hangs himself. This is important in that both Peter and Judas had <u>turned</u> from Jesus. The difference is that Judas never asked for forgiveness. The only way to make this clear, especially to those who have never read the bible, was to have Judas virtually at the foot of the cross... under the body of Jesus... feeling remorse; yet, <u>not asking for forgiveness</u>. Picking up the rope at the base of the cross, Judas walks away, obviously full of remorse, and hangs himself.

Matt. 26:21-26 And as they were eating, He said, ***"Truly I say to you that one of you will betray Me."*** *And being deeply grieved, they each one began to say to Him, "Surely not I, Lord?" And He answered and said,* ***"He who dipped his hand with Me in the bowl is the one who will betray Me. The Son of Man {is to} go, just as it is written of Him; but woe to that man by whom the Son of Man is betrayed! It would have been good for that man if he had not been born."*** *And Judas, who was betraying Him, answered and said, "Surely it is not I, Rabbi?" He said to him,* ***"You have said {it} yourself."***

Prov. 16:4 The LORD has made everything for its own purpose, Even the wicked for the day of evil.

Ps. 41:9 Even my close friend, in whom I trusted, <u>Who ate my bread</u>, Has lifted up his heel against me.

1Cor. 11:27 Therefore <u>whoever eats the bread or drinks the cup of the Lord in an unworthy manner,</u> shall be guilty of the body and the blood of the Lord.

1. Was Judas' repentance directed toward God and Jesus, or toward the chief priests and the elders?

> *Matt. 27:3-5   When <u>Judas</u>, His betrayer, <u>saw that Jesus was condemned</u>, he repented and brought back the thirty pieces of silver to the chief priests and the elders. He said, "I have sinned by betraying innocent blood." <u>But they said</u>, "What is that to us? See to it yourself." Throwing down the pieces of silver in the temple, he departed: and he went and hanged himself.*

> *2Cor. 7:10   For the sorrow that is according to {the will} {of} God produces a repentance without regret, {leading} to salvation; but <u>the sorrow of the world produces death.</u>*

> *Matt. 7:19-23   **"Every tree that does not bear good fruit is cut down and thrown into the fire. "So then, you will know them by their fruits.   "Not everyone who says to Me, 'Lord, Lord,' will enter the kingdom of heaven; but he who does the will of My Father who is in heaven.   "Many will say to Me on that day, 'Lord, Lord, did we not prophesy in Your name, and in Your name cast out demons, and in Your name perform many miracles?'   "And then I will declare to them, 'I never knew you; Go away from Me, you evildoers."***

> *John 17:12   **"While I was with them, I was keeping them in Thy name which Thou hast given Me; and I guarded them, and not one of them perished <u>but the son of perdition, that the Scripture might be fulfilled."</u>***

> *Acts 1:24-25   Then they prayed and said, "Lord, you know everyone's heart. Show us which one of these two You have chosen to take the place in this*

ministry and apostleship from which <u>Judas turned aside to go to his own place.</u>"

The lyrics of the song **"Did You Ever Hear The Story"** allow us to reflect once more on the humanity and love of Christ, and the foolishness of the world apart from Him.

Just as it was then, it's the same today. The world still has its lovers and its fools. Is it so hard to realize that the only price for true freedom, is Love? The love that Jesus offered all the way to the cross.... and still offers today, is everlasting and knows no boundaries, race or color.

> *Prov. 10:12 Hatred stirs up strife, But love covers all transgressions.*

> *1Pet. 4:8 Above all, keep fervent in your love for one another, because love covers a multitude of sins.*

As the song states: Do you want to hear a story of a world living together, or do you want to hear a story of how it ends?

> *Matt. 24:14* **"And this gospel of the kingdom shall be preached in the whole world for a witness to all the nations, and then the end shall come."**

The reason you never see Judas actually hang himself is because there are so many teen suicides taking place today by hanging. God loves you, and just because Judas chose that path certainly doesn't mean that it's okay, or the only way out. <u>There is forgiveness if you ask for it</u>.... Judas didn't .... Peter did.

It is not Judas' betrayal that put Jesus on the cross, rather, it was our sins.

NOTES:

EXT. FUNERAL PROCESSION. DAY: (SCENE 24)

                             (MOURNERS cry, walk behind JESSE's casket. PETER watches.)

                             (SONG **"FORGIVE ME"** PLAYS OVER ENTIRE SCENE)

                             (THE YOUNG PROSTITUTE... obviously changed, now dressed in white, carries a WREATH of DOGWOOD and walks alongside the casket)

                             (PETER faces off funeral, which is now approaching)

SONG LYRICS: (VO) WHO AM I
                             WHAT AM I SUPPOSED TO DO ...
                             TELL ME
                             HOW CAN I FACE TOMORROW ...
                             WITHOUT YOU

                             (PETER backs up and SHAKEN breathes heavy)

PETER: Heavy inhale and exhale sound.

SONG LYRICS: (VO) WHAT AM I
                             WHERE AM I SUPPOSED TO GO ...
                             TELL ME

PETER: Exhales.

SONG LYRICS: (VO) HOW CAN I LIVE WITHOUT YOU
                             WHEN YOU'RE WITHIN ME

EXT. BEACH NIGHT:

(FLASHBACK.)

PETER: And I'd never forsake you ... Never.

SONG LYRICS: (VO) FORGIVE ME
FOR ALL THE PAIN I PUT YOU
THROUGH
FOR ALL THE TIMES

EXT. FUNERAL PROCESSION. DAY:

PETER: (Screams over song) **J E S S E** !!

(The young PROSTITUTE, now turns
and looks at PETER)

SONG LYRICS: (VO) I DOUBTED YOU
FOR YOUR ONLY CRIME TO ME
WAS YOU LOVED ME
WITH A LOVE I'VE NEVER KNOWN
A LOVE I'LL NEVER KNOW AGAIN
'CAUSE I THREW AWAY THE
CHANCE

(PETER reaches for casket.
POLICEMAN HITS PETER.
PETER falls to ground.
CUNNINGHAM watches from window
of CUNNINGHAM'S HOME.   ANDY,
JAMES, JOHN run through crowd to
PETER,)

ANDY: Peter? Peter? Are you all right?

JAMES: Peter, where have you been? I thought
you were dead, man.

EXT. FUNERAL PROCESSION. DAY. (CONTINUED):

PETER: Take me home ... TAKE ME HOME!

STUDY SCENE:
NO. 24

In this scene we find ourselves in the midst of a funeral procession. A young girl, dressed in white, walks beside a wooden coffin and carries a wreath of dogwood. This is the same girl that we saw earlier in the film as a prostitute. It is obvious that her encounter with Jesse, changed her life; and, wearing white symbolizes her purity in heart.... just as He saw her.

> *Luke 7:44-48 And turning toward the woman, He said to Simon,* ***"Do you see this woman? I entered your house; you gave Me no water for My feet, but she has wet My feet with her tears, and wiped them with her hair. You gave Me no kiss; but she, since the time I came in, has not ceased to kiss My feet. You did not anoint My head with oil, but she anointed My feet with perfume.   For this reason I say to you, <u>her sins, which are many, have been forgiven,</u> for she loved much; but he who is forgiven little, loves little."*** *And He said to her,* ***"<u>Your sins have been forgiven.</u>"***
>
> *(Luke 7:50)* ***"Your faith has saved you; go in peace."***

As the song **"Forgive Me"** begins to build, we see Peter standing in the middle of the road facing the procession. His best friend, the Son of God ... everything he believes in is in that coffin.... fast approaching him. The lyrics of the song describe what Peter is feeling:

WHO AM I, WHAT AM I SUPPOSED TO DO?
TELL ME
HOW CAN I FACE TOMORROW WITHOUT YOU?

WHAT AM I, WHERE AM I SUPPOSED TO GO?
TELL ME

HOW CAN I LIVE WITHOUT YOU
WHEN YOU'RE WITHIN ME?

FORGIVE ME, FOR ALL THE PAIN I PUT YOU
THROUGH
FOR ALL THE TIMES I DOUBTED YOU
FOR YOUR ONLY CRIME TO ME
WAS YOU LOVED ME
WITH A LOVE I'VE NEVER KNOWN
A LOVE I'LL NEVER KNOW AGAIN
'CAUSE I THREW AWAY THE CHANCE.

The coffin draws nearer, and Peter has a flashback of his telling Jesse: "Jesse, I'll never forsake you." At that moment he reaches out and touches the coffin. <u>He has the power to heal and raise the dead</u>, but with all the gifts he possesses, he can't bring Jesse back nor can he undo his denying knowing him or running away..

> *Matt. 10:7-8 "**And as you go, preach, saying, 'The kingdom of heaven is at hand.' "Heal {the} sick, <u>raise {the} dead</u>, cleanse {the} lepers, cast out demons; freely you received, freely give.***

Peter feels like a total failure and the blow that strikes him from behind is a visual symbol of his helplessness, despair and the total separation from the humanity of his friend.

Cunningham watches from his balcony as the funeral procession passes by. Recalling a previous encounter with Jesse, once again .... he grabs his wrist and turns away.

> *2Cor. 4:4 in whose case the god of this world has blinded the minds of the unbelieving, that they might not see the light of the gospel of the glory of Christ, who is the image of God.*

As the scene ends Peter, now on his knees, is briefly consoled by people as they pass by. John, James and Andy approach

Peter expressing relief to see him as they thought he'd been killed during the storm. Peter, totally dejected, just wants to go home.

How many of us, like Peter, have found ourselves knocked down to our knees just wanting to go home?   Peter's missing a hand represents a physical handicap yet symbolic of the handicap in so many of our hearts. Fear is a paralyzing handicap that can maim you for life if you let it.   It destroys hope and will cripple your spirit ... and your faith.   God sees through our handicaps and into our heart. For it's there , in the heart, that we enter the crucible.... a place of refinement where the dross of our life is removed. <u>No one can go through the crucible for you</u>. It's <u>your</u> character that is being reshaped and <u>your</u> faith being strengthened.

> *John 15:1-5 **"I am the true vine, and My Father is the vinedresser.   Every branch in Me that does not bear fruit, He takes away; and every {branch} that bears fruit, He prunes it, that it may bear more fruit.   You are already clean because of the word which I have spoken to you.   Abide in Me, and I in you. As the branch cannot bear fruit of itself, unless it abides in the vine, so neither {can} you, unless you abide in Me.   I am the vine, you are the branches; he who abides in Me, and I in him, he bears much fruit; for apart from Me you can do nothing."***
>
> *John 15:7-9 **"If you abide in Me, and My words abide in you, ask whatever you wish, and it shall be done for you.   By this is My Father glorified, that you bear much fruit, and {so} prove to be My disciples.   Just as the Father has loved Me, I have also loved you; abide in My love."***

God patiently waits for us to get up off our knees, dust ourselves off and let the healing process begin.

NOTES:

INT. SUBURBAN. DAY: (SCENE 25)

                 (JOHN drives PETER, JAMES, ANDY.)

                 (SONG **"JESSE I NEED YOU"**
PLAYS OVER ENTIRE SCENE)

SONG LYRICS: (VO) JESSE I NEED YOU

EXT. RIVER. DAY:

                 (FLASHBACK, JESSE "fishes" with
JAMES. JAMES explaining his FLY
technique in background to JESSE.)

SONG LYRICS: (VO) I CAN'T BELIEVE YOU'D GO
AND LEAVE ME
I KNOW IT'S TRUE ... CAUSE IT'S
JUST LIKE YOU

YOU'VE ALWAYS BEEN A
WARRIOR
RUNNING OFF TO LEAD THE
BATTLE
I SHOULD HAVE KNOWN
YOU'D TAKE THE BATTLE HOME

AND NOW I'M FEELING LIKE A
CHILD
THAT YOU ONCE TOOK BY THE
HAND
AND I HEARD YOU SAY
A CHILD MUST BE A MAN
AND GIVE MORE ... THAN HE
FEELS ... HE CAN

                 (ANDY pushes JOHN into water.)

EXT. RIVER. DAY (CONT'D):

JOHN: Woa! Ah! Hey! Etc.

JAMES: What're you doing? You're gonna scare
                    all my fish away!!

SONG LYRICS: (VO) JESSE, I LOVE YOU
                    I CAN'T BELIEVE HOW MUCH I
                    MISS YOU

                    (JAMES pulls fish out of water.)

JAMES: Ah..HA!

                    (ALL laugh.)

SONG LYRICS: (VO) YOU WERE ALWAYS THERE
                    WHEN I NEEDED YOU

INT. SUBURBAN. DAY:

SONG LYRICS: (VO) SO, I GUESS I'LL BE A
                    WARRIOR
                    RUNNING OFF TO LEAD THE
                    BATTLE
                    LIKE YOU KNEW I COULD
                    LIKE YOU KNEW I WOULD

                    AND WHEN I FEEL LIKE GOING
                    HOME

EXT. MOUNTAIN SIDE. DAY:

                    (FLASHBACK over song.)

JOHN: I know who you are

EXT. MOUNTAIN SIDE. DAY (CONT'D):

SONG LYRICS: (VO) I'LL, ALWAYS HEAR YOU

JESSE: Who am I JOHN?

SONG LYRICS: (VO) ON THE PHONE

JOHN: You're a great teacher ...

SONG LYRICS: (VO) THERE'LL BE TIMES

JOHN CONT'D: and a healer.

INT. SUBURBAN DAY:

SONG LYRICS: (VO) GOD CALLS A MAN ...
TO BE MORE ... THAN HE FEELS HE
CAN

EXT. RIVER. DAY:

(FLASHBACK. PETER approaches
JUDAS.)

PETER: Hey friend, you wish you were back in
New York now?

JUDAS: What are you, nuts?

INT. SUBURBAN DAY:

SONG LYRICS: (VO) JESSE, I NEED YOU
I CAN'T BELIEVE YOU'D GO AND
LEAVE ME
I KNOW IT'S TRUE

EXT. CAMPFIRE. NIGHT:

(FLASHBACK over song)

(JESSE hands ANDY coffee mug.)

ANDY:	Thanks.
SONG LYRICS:	(VO) CAUSE IT'S JUST LIKE ...
ANDY:	Jesse ...
SONG LYRICS:	(VO) YOU
ANDY:	Teach me how to pray?
JESSE:	There's no formula. Just don't pray with your mind ... pray with your heart.
ANDY:	OK.
JESSE:	OK.

STUDY SCENE:
NO. 25

This scene brings out the bond of friendship between Jesse and his disciples as well as their humanity. Throughout the film we have seen Jesse perform miracles, and confront the heart of man.

Jesus and His disciples did not teach and/or minister 24 hrs. a day. There was a time to rest and a time to fellowship with each other. Fishing was one thing they all enjoyed and had in common; however, as this scene points out, fly fishing isn't quite the same as net fishing.

James has only a smattering of an idea of how to fly fish. Jesse caringly listens as James tries to explain and teach Him how to catch a fish... that He created. Jesse, having a sense of humor, makes the trout take the bait and chuckles as James, now full of himself, sets the hook and begins to show off. Any fly fisherman knows that when you hang a fish, you don't turn loose of the slack line .... you keep it tight and work the fish in. James, on the other hand turns it all loose and starts cranking for all he's worth.

It wasn't James' skill that helped him catch the fish, it was due to his persistence that God cared enough about him person-ally, to intervene on his behalf. Sometimes God will put a fish on your line just to rekindle hope and trust in Him to let you know... He's always there (with you).

John recalls the early times when he only saw Jesse as a great teacher and healer. One can't help but wonder how many people in this world still think about Jesus the same way.

Andy reflects on a fundamental need that is of utmost importance to us all. He asks Jesse; "Teach Me How To Pray" (or how to communicate with God). Jesse responds; "There's no formula ... Just don't pray with your mind, pray with your heart."

1. Jesus had a lot to show us about prayer, mostly to be real with God and speak from the heart (inner room).

> *Matt. 6:5-8* **"And when you pray, you are not to be as the hypocrites; for they love to stand and pray in the synagogues and on the street corners, in order to be seen by men. Truly I say to you, they have their reward in full. But you, when you pray, go into your inner room, and when you have shut your door, pray to your Father who is in secret, and your Father who sees in secret will repay you. And when you are praying, do not use meaningless repetition, as the Gentiles do, for they suppose that they will be heard for their many words. Therefore do not be like them; for your Father knows what you need, before you ask Him."**

2. Jesus gave us a model, a guide as to how we should pray. To us it is known as "The Lord's Prayer".

> *Matt. 6:9-13* **"Pray, then, in this way: Our Father who art in heaven, Hallowed be Thy name. 'Thy kingdom come. Thy will be done, On earth as it is in heaven. Give us this day our daily bread. And forgive us our debts, as we also have forgiven our debtors. And do not lead us into temptation, but deliver us from evil. [For Thine is the kingdom, and the power, and the glory, forever. Amen.]'"**

3. Jesus goes further to stress the importance of forgiveness.

> *Matt. 6:14-15* **"For if you forgive men for their transgressions, your heavenly Father will also forgive you. But if you do not forgive men, then your Father will not forgive your transgressions."**

If we can learn to pray with our hearts and talk to God as we would talk with a best friend, we would have a better relationship with Him. Remember, it's not formulas for prayer that God is interested in, <u>it's simply that we spend that special time with Him</u>... as a friend and <u>from the heart</u>.

As we read through the bible, the humanity of Jesus and His disciples, as well as their friendship is of paramount importance if we are truly to better understand Gods love for us. He doesn't want to separate Himself from us and be aloof, rather interact with us showing that He cares and is always there for us. That's why God sent His Son, to nurture us, teach us, show us more of Himself. Jesus was someone you could touch, put your arms around, walk with, fish with, eat with (He even cooked for the disciples). He was a man... a God-man ... His two natures bound together in such a way that the two become one having a single consciousness and Will, yet subject to the same hunger, thirst, weariness, pain, sorrow, laughter, anger, tears, temptation and all the other qualities and frailties that make up a human being... and yet ... He was without sin.

1. The humanity of Jesus Christ is seen in His human parentage:

> *Matt. 2:11   And they came into the house and saw the Child (Jesus) with Mary His mother;*
>
> *Luke 2:39   And when they {his parents, Mary and Joseph} had performed everything according to the Law of the Lord {circumsizion}, they returned to Galilee, to their own city of Nazareth.*

2. Jesus developed as a normal human being.

> *Luke 2:40   And the Child continued to grow and become strong, increasing in wisdom; and the grace of God was upon Him.*

> *Luke 2:41-52   And His parents used to go to Jerusalem every year at the Feast of the Passover. <u>And when He became twelve,</u> they went up {there} according to the custom of the Feast;   and as they were returning, after spending the full number of days, the boy Jesus stayed behind in Jerusalem. And His parents were unaware of it, but supposed Him to be in the caravan, and went a day's journey; and they {began} looking for Him among their relatives and acquaintances. And when they did not find Him, they returned to Jerusalem, looking for Him. And it came about that <u>after three days they found Him</u> in the temple, sitting in the midst of the teachers, both listening to them, and asking them questions. And all who heard Him were amazed at His understanding and His answers. And when they saw Him, they were astonished; and His mother said to Him, "Son, why have You treated us this way? Behold, Your father and I have been anxiously looking for You." And He said to them, **<u>"Why is it that you were looking for Me? Did you not know that I had to be in My Father's {house?"}</u>**   And they did not understand the statement which He had made to them.   <u>And He went down with them, and came to Nazareth; and He continued in subjection to them;</u> and His mother treasured all {these} things in her heart. And Jesus kept increasing in wisdom and stature, and in favor with God and men.*

A. Jesus grew up at home with his brothers and sisters.

> *Matt. 13:55-56 "Is not this the carpenter's son? Is not His mother called Mary, and His brothers, James and Joseph and Simon and Judas? And His sisters, are they not all with us?"*

B. Those who had known Jesus from childhood, <u>even members of His family</u>, had a hard time accepting and honoring His wisdom, and miraculous powers.

> *Matt. 13:54-58 And coming to His home town He {began} teaching them in their synagogue, so that they became astonished, and said, "Where {did} this man {get} this wisdom, and {these} miraculous powers? "Is not this the carpenter's son? Is not His mother called Mary, and His brothers, James and Joseph and Simon and Judas? "And His sisters, are they not all with us? Where then {did} this man {get} all these things?" <u>And they took offense at Him.</u> But Jesus said to them, **<u>"A prophet is not without honor except in his home town, and in his {own} household."</u>** And He did not do many miracles there because of their <u>unbelief</u>.*

3. As a man, and like each of us, Jesus experienced:

   A. Hunger

   > *Matt. 21:18 Now in the morning, when He returned to the city, He became hungry.*

   B. Thirst

   > *John 4:7 There came a woman of Samaria to draw water. Jesus said to her, **"Give Me a drink."***

   C. Weariness

   > *John 4:6   Jesus therefore, being wearied from His journey, was sitting thus by the well.*

   D. Tears

   > *John 11:35 Jesus wept.*

   > *Luke 19:41 And when He approached, He saw the city and wept over it, ...*

E. Temptation

> *Hebr. 4:15 For we do not have a high priest who cannot sympathize with our weaknesses, but One who has been tempted in all things as {we are, yet} without sin.*

F. Cooking

> *John 21:9 And so when they got out upon the land they saw a charcoal fire {already} laid, and fish placed on it, and bread.*
>
> *John 21:12 Jesus said to them,* **"Come {and} have breakfast."**

G. Anger

> *Matt. 21:12 And Jesus entered the temple and cast out all those who were buying and selling in the temple, and overturned the tables of the money-changers and the seats of those who were selling doves.*

H. Laughter (outward expression of joy)

> *Prov. 17:22 A joyful heart is good medicine.*
>
> *Luke 6:21* **Blessed {are} you who weep now, for you shall laugh.**

I. Need For Rest

> *John 12:36   He departed and hid Himself from them (the multitude).*
>
> *Mark 6:31-32 And He said to them,* **"Come away by yourselves to a lonely place and rest a while."** *(For there were many {people} coming and going,*

and they did not even have time to eat.)   And they went away in the boat to a lonely place by themselves.

J. The Need To Pray

Mark 6:46   He departed to the mountain to pray.

Luke 5:16   But He Himself would {often} slip away to the wilderness and pray.

Luke 6:12   And it was at this time that He went off to the mountain to pray, and He spent the whole night in prayer to God.

4. Jesus knew the importance of touch and our need to touch Him.

Luke 6:19   <u>And all the multitude were trying to touch Him</u>, for power was coming from Him and healing {them} all.

*Mark 10:14   **"Permit the children to <u>come to Me</u>; do not hinder them; for the kingdom of God belongs to such as these."***

John 13:23   There was <u>reclining on Jesus' breast</u> one of His disciples, whom Jesus loved. (John)

Luke 18:15-16 People were bringing even infants to him that <u>He might touch them;</u>

5. There is healing in His touch and in our reaching/believing and touching Him.

Mark 5:25-42 And a woman who had had a hemor-

*rhage for twelve years, and had endured much at the hands of many physicians, and had spent all that she had and was not helped at all, but rather had grown worse, after hearing about Jesus, came up in the crowd behind {Him,} <u>and touched His cloak</u>. For she thought, "<u>If I just touch His garments, I shall get well.</u>" And immediately the flow of her blood was dried up; and she felt in her body that she was healed of her affliction. And immediately Jesus, perceiving in Himself that the power {proceeding} from Him had gone forth, turned around in the crowd and said, "**<u>Who touched My garments?</u>**" And His disciples said to Him, "You see the multitude pressing in on You, and You say, '<u>Who touched Me?</u>'" And He looked around to see the woman who had done this. But the woman fearing and trembling, aware of what had happened to her, came and fell down before Him, and told Him the whole truth. And He said to her, "**Daughter, your faith has made you well; go in peace, and be healed of your affliction.**" While He was still speaking, they came from the {house of} the synagogue official, saying, "Your daughter has died; why trouble the Teacher anymore?" But Jesus, overhearing what was being spoken, said to the synagogue official, "**Do not be afraid {any} {longer,} only believe.**" And He allowed no one to follow with Him, except Peter and James and John the brother of James. And they came to the house of the synagogue official; and He beheld a commotion, and {people} loudly weeping and wailing. And entering in, He said to them, "**Why make a commotion and weep? The child has not died, but is asleep.**" And they {began} laughing at Him. But putting them all out, He took along the child's father and mother and His own companions, and entered {the room} where the child was. <u>And taking the child by the hand,</u> He said to her, "**Talitha kum!**" (**which translated means, "Little girl, I say** *to you, arise!"). And immediately the girl rose and {began} to walk; for she was twelve years old. And immediately they were completely astounded.*

6. His door is always open and there's always room at His table ... even for sinners.

> *Matt. 9:10-12 And it happened that as He was reclining {at the table} in the house, behold many tax-gatherers and sinners came and were dining with Jesus and His disciples. And when the Pharisees saw {this,} they said to His disciples, "Why is your Teacher eating with the tax-gatherers and sinners?" But when He heard this, He said, " {It is} not those who are healthy who need a physician, but those who are sick.*

7. Jesus always made Himself available to those who sought Him. It came natural to Him as that's why He came ... to seek out and save that which is lost.

> *Luke 19:1-10 And He entered and was passing through Jericho. And behold, there was a man called by the name of Zaccheus; and he was a chief tax-gatherer, and he was rich. And he was trying to see who Jesus was, and he was unable because of the crowd, for he was small in stature. And he ran on ahead and climbed up into a sycamore tree in order to see Him, for He was about to pass through that way. And when Jesus came to the place, He looked up and said to him, "Zaccheus, hurry and come down, for today I must stay at your house." And he hurried and came down, and received Him gladly. And when they saw it, they all {began} to grumble, saying, "He has gone to be the guest of a man who is a sinner." And Zaccheus stopped and said to the*

Lord, "Behold, Lord, half of my possessions I will give to the poor, and if I have defrauded anyone of anything, I will give back four times as much." And Jesus said to him, **"Today salvation has come to this house, because he, too, is a son of Abraham. "For the Son of Man has come to seek and to save that which was lost."**

As depicted in this scene, the disciples find themselves seemingly alone with their memories and without the companionship of their departed friend. The song **"Jesse I Need You"** takes you into their hearts and exposes their inner feelings.

JESSE I NEED YOU
I CAN'T BELIEVE YOU'D GO AND LEAVE ME
I KNOW IT'S TRUE, 'CAUSE IT'S JUST LIKE YOU.
YOU'VE ALWAYS BEEN A WARRIOR
RUNNING OFF TO LEAD THE BATTLE
I SHOULD HAVE KNOWN,
YOU'D TAKE THE BATTLE HOME.

AND NOW I'M FEELING LIKE THE CHILD
THAT YOU ONCE TOOK BY THE HAND
AND I HEARD YOU SAY, A CHILD MUST BE A MAN
AND GIVE MORE THAN HE FEELS HE CAN.

JESSE I LOVE YOU
I CAN'T BELIEVE HOW MUCH I MISS YOU
YOU WERE ALWAYS THERE,
WHEN I NEEDED YOU

SO I GUESS I'LL BE A WARRIOR,
RUNNING OFF TO LEAD THE BATTLE
LIKE YOU KNEW I COULD,
LIKE YOU KNEW I WOULD.

AND WHEN I FEEL LIKE GOING HOME
I'LL ALWAYS HEAR YOU ON THE PHONE

THERE'LL BE TIMES GOD CALLS A MAN
TO GIVE MORE THAN HE FEELS HE CAN.

JESSE I NEED YOU
I CAN'T BELIEVE YOU'D GO AND LEAVE ME
I KNOW IT'S TRUE, 'CAUSE IT'S JUST LIKE YOU.

Jesus is, and always will be, our friend and advocate. When you pray, it may help to picture yourself with Him ... sitting together.... or walking together; or, enjoying your favorite hobby or sport together. Choose to let Him be part of your everyday life and share your heart with Him as if He is your best friend.... because He is.

> *Hebr. 13:5 ... for He has said,* **"I will never leave you or forsake you."**

> *Matt. 28:20 ... "And remember, I am with you always, even to the end of the age."*

There is no "formula" for sharing your heart.... only honesty and simplicity. Share your good times and bad times, laughter and tears. And when you have finished, learn to wait for His response.

NOTES:

EXT. BEACH. EARLY MORNING: (SCENE 26)

                    (SONG **"ONLY THEN"** PLAYS
                    OVER THE ENTIRE SCENE)

                    (SUNRISE ... PETER walks along the
                    beach by the ocean.)

SONG LYRICS: (VO) WHEN YOUR EYES CAN SEE
                    AS I SEE
                    AND YOUR HEART CAN FOLLOW
                    MY DREAM
                    AND YOU LIVE FOR THE LIFE
                    THAT'S IN ME
                    ONLY THEN COULD YOU EVER
                    KNOW ME
                    ONLY THEN COULD YOU EVER
                    LOVE ME

                    (Various FLASHBACKS seen under
                    song. NO DIALOGUE overlaps.)

SONG LYRICS: (VO) WHEN YOU COME TO THE
                    DUSK OF YOUR DREAMS
                    AND YOU TAKE ALL THE PAIN
                    LOVE CAN BRING
                    AND YOU STILL LOVE WITH THE
                    LOVE THAT'S IN ME
                    ONLY THEN COULD YOU EVER
                    KNOW ME
                    ONLY THEN COULD YOU EVER
                    LOVE ME

PETER: (OS) Forgive me! **Forgive me**!
                    (PETER hears a voice behind him)

JESSE: (OS) **DO YOU LOVE ME**?

EXT. BEACH. EARLY MORNING (CONT'D):

> (PETER sees JESSE RESURRECT in front of his eyes ... as what was a bright glow turns into a human form)

SONG LYRICS: (VO) WHEN YOU LOVE WITH THE LOVE IN MY HEART

> (PETER and JESSE embrace in a bear hug... as PETER is forgiven.)

SONG LYRICS: (VO) ONLY THEN COULD YOU EVER KNOW ME

> (FREEZE FRAME and START SLOW PULL AWAY)

SONG LYRICS: (VO) ONLY THEN COULD YOU EVER LOVE ME

> (Continue PULL AWAY until FADE OUT)

> (END CREDITS ROLL OVER BLACK.)

**** THE END ****

STUDY SCENE:
NO. 26

A new day is dawning and we see Peter walking alone by the sea. He is full of remorse and greatly pained over what he's done. As he drops to his knees and slowly lets the sand sift through his fingers, his mind rages war with his heart. Knowing the full weight of his denial, he recalls the gentle and reassuring touch of Jesse's hand upon his face.

Thinking back to the crucifixion, a mental picture, of Jesse being hoisted up the cross with his arms outstretched toward him and the others, burns in his mind. The look in Jesse's eyes tugs at Peter's heart, for it is a look not of reproach or condemnation; rather one of compassion, understanding and pain overshadowed by love. As the nails pierce Jesse's flesh Peter feels an even greater pain ripping through his soul .. the realization of the shallowness of his love as compared to the depth of Jesse's.

As Peter recalls reaching out to touch Jesse's coffin, he knows Jesse's dead but can't accept it ... he can't let him go. He not only needs to forgive himself ... he desperately needs God's forgiveness.

It's then that Peter stands up, throws the sand to the ground and cries out to God; Forgive me! Forgive me!

As a bright light flashes behind him, he hears a familiar voice; Do you love me? Peter turns around and, stunned, finds himself face to face with Jesse.

As the two men "hug" each other, Peter knows he's forgiven. His friend, Lord and Savior ... the Son of God ..., **has risen from the dead** just as He had said He would.

1. Jesus Is Risen:

> *Acts 10:40-41 God raised Him up on the third day, and granted that He should become visible, not to all the people, but to witnesses who were chosen beforehand by God, {that is,} to us, who ate and drank with Him after He arose from the dead.*

> *Matt. 28:1-10 Now after the Sabbath, as it began to dawn toward the first {day} of the week, Mary Magdalene and the other Mary came to look at the grave. And behold, a severe earthquake had occurred, for an angel of the Lord descended from heaven and came and rolled away the stone and sat upon it. And his appearance was like lightning, and his garment as white as snow; and the guards shook for fear of him, and became like dead men. And the angel answered and said to the women, "Do not be afraid; for I know that you are looking for Jesus who has been crucified. "He is not here, for He has risen, just as He said. Come, see the place where He was lying. "And go quickly and tell His disciples that He has risen from the dead; and behold, He is going before you into Galilee, there you will see Him; behold, I have told you."   And they departed quickly from the tomb with fear and great joy and ran to report it to His disciples. And behold, Jesus met them and greeted them. And they came up and took hold of His feet and worshiped Him. Then Jesus said to them, **"Do not be afraid; go and take word to My brethren to leave for Galilee, and there they shall see Me."***

2. The Chief Priest Fabricate Lies About Jesus's Resurrection:

> *Matt. 28:11-15 Now while they were on their way, behold, some of the guard came into the city*

and reported to the chief priests all that had happened. And when they had assembled with the elders and counseled together, they gave a large sum of money to the soldiers, and said, "You are to say, 'His disciples came by night and stole Him away while we were asleep.' And if this should come to the governor's ears, we will win him over and keep you out of trouble." And they took the money and did as they had been instructed; and this story was widely spread among the Jews, {and is} to this day.

3. Disciples Refuse To Believe Jesus Has Risen:

*Mark 16:9-15 [Now after He had risen early on the first day of the week, He first appeared to Mary Magdalene, from whom He had cast out seven demons. She went and reported to those who had been with Him, while they were mourning and weeping. And when they heard that He was alive, and had been seen by her, <u>they refused to believe it</u>. And after that, He appeared in a different form to two of them, while they were walking along on their way to the country. And they went away and reported it to the others, <u>but they did not believe them either.</u> And afterward He appeared to the eleven themselves as they were reclining {at the table;} and <u>He reproached them for their unbelief and hardness of heart, because they had not believed those who had seen Him after He had risen.</u> And He said to them, **"Go into all the world and preach the gospel to all creation."***

*Luke 24:38-47 And He said to them, **"<u>Why are you troubled, and why do doubts arise in your hearts?</u> See My hands and My feet, that it is I***

Myself; touch Me and see, for a spirit does not have flesh and bones as you see that I have." [*And when He had said this, He showed them His hands and His feet.*] *And while they still could not believe {it} for joy and were marveling, He said to them,* **"Have you anything here to eat?"** *And they gave Him a piece of a broiled fish; and He took it and ate {it} before them. Now He said to them,* **"These are My words which I spoke to you while I was still with you, that all things which are written about Me in the Law of Moses and the Prophets and the Psalms must be fulfilled."**

4. Jesus Opens Their Minds:

Luke 24: 45-47 Then He opened their minds to understand the Scriptures, and He said to them, **"Thus it is written, that the Christ should suffer and rise again from the dead the third day; and that repentance for forgiveness of sins should be proclaimed in His name to all the nations, beginning from Jerusalem."**

5. They Receive The Holy Spirit:

John 20:21 Jesus therefore said to them again, **"Peace {be} with you; as the Father has sent Me, I also send you."** *And when He had said this, He breathed on them, and said to them,* **"Receive the Holy Spirit. If you forgive the sins of any, {their sins} have been forgiven them; if you retain the {sins} of any, they have been retained."**

6. Their witness wasn't enough for Thomas. He needed solid proof ... something he could see and touch.

> *John 20:25-29   So the other disciples told him, "We have seen the Lord." But he (Thomas) said to them, "Unless I see the mark of the nails in his hands, and put my finger in the mark of the nails and my hand in his side, I will not believe." A week later his disciples were again in the house, and Thomas was with them. Although the doors were shut, Jesus came and stood among them and said, **"Peace be with you."** Then he said to Thomas, **"Put your finger here and see my hands. Reach out your hand and put it in my side. <u>Do not doubt but believe.</u>"** Thomas answered him, "My Lord and my God!" Jesus said to him, **"Because you have seen Me, have you believed? Blessed {are} they who did not see, and {yet} believed."***

6. <u>After His resurrection, Jesus asks Peter</u>: "Do You Love Me?"

> *John 21:15   So when they had finished breakfast, Jesus said to Simon Peter, **"Simon, {son} of John, do you love Me more than these?"** He said to Him, "Yes, Lord; You know that I love You." He said to him, **"<u>Tend My lambs</u>."***

> *John 21:16   He said to him again a second time, **"Simon, {son} of John, do you love Me?"** He said to Him, "Yes, Lord; You know that I love You." He said to him, **"<u>Shepherd My sheep</u>."***

> *John 21:17   He said to him the third time, **"Simon, {son} of John, do you love Me?"** Peter was grieved because He said to him the third time, **"Do you love Me?"** And he said to Him, "Lord, You know all things; You know that I love You."*

*Jesus said to him, "**Tend My sheep**."*

A. When Jesus told Peter to **"tend"** and **"shepherd"** His
sheep, He was also telling Peter to be prepared to lay down
his life for them if he truly loves Him/them.

> *John 10:11-18 "**I am the good shepherd; the good
> shepherd lays down His life for the sheep.   He
> who is a hireling, and not a shepherd, who is not
> the owner of the sheep, beholds the wolf coming,
> and leaves the sheep, and flees, and the wolf
> snatches them, and scatters {them.}   { He flees}
> because he is a hireling, and is not concerned about
> the sheep. I am the good shepherd; and I know
> My own, and My own know Me,   even as the
> Father knows Me and I know the Father; and I lay
> down My life for the sheep. And I have other
> sheep, which are not of this fold; I must bring them
> also, and they shall hear My voice; and they shall
> become one flock {with} one shepherd.   For this
> reason the Father loves Me, because I lay down
> My life that I may take it again. No one has taken
> it away from Me, but I lay it down on My own
> initiative. I have authority to lay it down, and I
> have authority to take it up again. This command-
> ment I received from My Father.*"

> *John 15:13 "**Greater love has no one than this,
> that one lay down his life for his friends**."*

7. Jesus Ascends:

> *Acts 1:9-11 And after He had said these things,
> He was lifted up while they were looking on, and <u>a
> cloud received Him </u>out of their sight. And as they*

were gazing intently into the sky while He was departing, behold, two men in white clothing stood beside them;   and they also said, "Men of Galilee, why do you stand looking into the sky? This Jesus, who has been taken up from you into heaven, <u>will come in just the same way as you have watched Him go into heaven.</u>"

Mark 16:19 ... He was received up into heaven, and sat down at the right hand of God.

Through the lyrics in the song, we listen in to the message God is writing not only in Peter's heart but our hearts as well:

WHEN YOUR EYES CAN <u>SEE AS I SEE</u>
AND YOUR HEART CAN <u>FOLLOW MY DREAM</u>
AND YOU LIVE FOR <u>THE LIFE THAT'S IN ME</u>
ONLY THEN, COULD YOU EVER <u>KNOW</u> ME
ONLY THEN, COULD YOU EVER <u>LOVE</u> ME

WHEN YOU COME TO THE DUSK OF YOUR DREAMS.
AND YOU TAKE ALL THE PAIN LOVE CAN BRING
AND YOU STILL LOVE WITH THE LOVE THAT'S IN ME
ONLY THEN COULD YOU EVER KNOW ME
ONLY THEN COULD YOU EVER LOVE ME

WHEN YOU LOVE WITH THE LOVE IN MY HEART
ONLY THEN, COULD YOU EVER KNOW ME
ONLY THEN, COULD YOU EVER LOVE ME.

Jesus has provided the way for us to roll away the stone from the doorway of our own heart. He gently speaks:

*Rev. 3: 20   **"Behold, I stand at the door and knock; if anyone hears My voice and opens the door, I will come in to him, and will dine with*** *him, and he with Me."*

Ezek. 11:19-20   "And I shall give them one heart, and shall put a new spirit within them. And I shall take the heart of stone out of their flesh and give them a heart of flesh,   that they may walk in My statutes and keep My ordinances, and do them. Then they will be My people, and I shall be their God."

*Matt. 28:18-20   "**All authority has been given to Me in heaven and on earth.   Go therefore and make disciples of all the nations, baptizing them in the name of the Father and the Son and the Holy Spirit,   teaching them to observe all that I commanded you; and lo, I am with you always, even to the end of the age.**"*

*What If
The Dusk Of A Dream
Was The Dawn
Of A Vision?*

JBE

NOTES

For information regarding the availability of Mr. and Mrs. Barden for:

Speaking Engagements
Guest Appearances
&
Consulting

Please Contact:

James Barden Planning and Mgt., Inc.
4508 South Laburnum Avenue
Richmond, Virginia . 23231-2422
Tel: (804) 222-4180
Fax: (804) 236-0133

For information regarding future books to be released by Mr. and Mrs. Barden:

Please Contact:

Barrington & Walstone, Publishers
P.O. Box 959
Shallotte, N.C. 28459

Toll Free: (888) 777-2671   Pin No. 5949

To order your copy of "THE JUDAS PROJECT":

1. MOTION PICTURE VIDEO
2. MOTION PICTURE SOUNDTRACK
    Available on CD and CASSETTE

SIMPLY CALL ... FOR <u>IMMEDIATE DELIVERY</u>:
Toll Free: (888) 777-2671   Pin No. 5949

Mastercard and Visa are accepted.

OR

ASK FOR THEM AT YOUR LOCAL
CHRISTIAN BOOKSTORE

SOUNDTRACK & MOTION PICTURE VIDEO DISTRIBUTED BY:

ROCKY MOUNTAIN ENTERTAINMENT, INC.
and
SPRING ARBOR DISTRIBUTORS, INC.